WHY? Children's Questions

Books by the authors

Charting Intellectual Development: A Practical Guide to
Piagetian Tasks

WHY? Children's Questions: What They Mean and How to
Answer Them

WHY? Children's Questions

What They Mean and How to
Answer Them

Ruth Formanek and Anita Gurian

Houghton Mifflin Company Boston 1980

Library of Congress Cataloging in Publication Data
Formanek, Ruth.
   Why? Children's Questions

   Includes bibliographical references.
    1. Cognition in children.   2. Curiosity in children.   3. Parent and child.   4. Children—Management.   I. Gurian, Anita, joint author.   II. Title.
BF723.C5F68   155.4'13   80–11382
ISBN 0–395–29190–9

Printed in the United States of America

S 10 9 8 7 6 5 4 3 2 1

Acknowledgments

WE THANK our collaborators — those children who questioned their parents and those parents who shared the questions with us. We thank our own children, friends, students, and colleagues who contributed to our project, in particular Caryl Bank, Betty Brooks, Sylvia Carter, Peter Favaro, Deborah Finkel, Richard Flaste, Douglas and Russell Gellman, Roger Goddard, Margot Karras, Doris Kertzner, Marilyn Maxwell, Ruth Nemtzow, Mary Ann Pulaski, Mary Anne Raywid, Tamara Schroeder, Barbara Smolens, Ina Zoob, Toni Liebman, Director of the Roslyn-Trinity Cooperative Day School, its parents, teachers, and children, and research assistants Lou Gallagher and Tom Moyer.

We are particularly grateful to Selma Greenberg for her critical reading of the manuscript and her valuable comments. Frances Tenenbaum contributed the encouragement, judgment, and guidance that are the special mark of a talented editor.

Contents

WHY? Children's Questions

Introduction

THE PSYCHOLOGIST David Elkind tells the story of driving in the car with his five-year-old son, when the boy asked, "If we keep driving will we come to the end of the earth?" The father's first inclination was to respond with the truth as he knew it, that the earth is round and therefore one cannot drive off, because there is no end. But knowing a thing or two about the way that most five-year-olds think, he caught himself. That would be a useless answer.

The roundness of the earth is logical enough to adults, of course; they watch ships disappear over the horizon and even have pictorial evidence in the form of photographs. However, from what is now known about the growth of thinking ability, thanks in large measure to the work of the Swiss psychologist Jean Piaget, it is apparent that logical arguments and evidence such as plastic globes cannot be convincing to five-year-olds. The mind of a five-year-old is pre-Columbian; the child depends on what is immediately visible — the earth is flat, no matter what you say. So David Elkind told his son, "Well, when you come to the end of the land there is water, and when you come to the end of the water you arrive at some more land." A lovely answer, conceptually within the grasp of the child and at the same time rigorously accurate.

Still, Elkind was lucky that time. Children, as it happens,

can ask much harder questions than that one. Very frequently they ask the kinds of questions that touch on a parent's deepest sense of self: one's own values, fears, and loves. They ask about sex and God and death.

The questions on sex alone can come in a creative way: What's the difference between boys and girls? Where do babies come from? Do boy babies get born from fathers? Daddy, when you were little were you a boy or a girl? And children often ask questions in bewilderingly rapid fire. Research shows that three-year-olds ask more than three hundred questions a day. This is a far cry from the number allotted to children by Lewis Carroll:

> "I have answered three questions, and that is enough,"
> Said his father. "Don't give yourself airs!
> Do you think I can listen all day to such stuff?
> Be off, or I'll kick you downstairs!"

Once all that inquisitiveness wouldn't have mattered much. Questioning children were considered garrulous, if not ill-mannered. Although it was only a generation or so ago that people were still saying that children should be seen and not heard, that notion now seems antique. In the nineteen-fifties, as Freudian thinking became widely popularized and parents became sensitized to the importance of those early, formative years, the pendulum began its swing. Parents, eager to protect their children's psyches and overalert to the detrimental effects on personality of frustration and inhibition, began to hang on the child's every word. Eagerness to stimulate learning and to respect the child as an individual are worthy trends, certainly, but when carried to extremes may result in a parent worn to a frazzle, exasperated, and filled with feelings of inadequacy.

In their desire to explain, parents often overwhelm youngsters with information. There was, for example, the three-year-old interviewed by the Russian writer Nicolai Chukovsky, who asked his father about the workings of a telephone: "Daddy, when you talk to me on the telephone, how do you get in there?" His father, a physicist — unfortunately in this case, since he actually knew how telephones work — undertook to explain the structure of the telephone.

The boy waited patiently through his father's explanation and then asked the question that, in his system, logically followed his first one: "But when you're finished talking, how do you crawl out again?" He had ignored his father's answer and stayed within his own system. That's what often happens. An inappropriate answer glances off the child's mind without making any noticeable impression, and most often doing no real harm. It can leave parents tired and frustrated, but maybe, if they still have a sense of humor, laughing.

Sometimes, however, children transform the answer into something they can deal with, something that fits into a concept they are already familiar with. For example, when told that a baby is inside the mother, many four-year-olds assume, on the basis of their experience, that she has eaten it. Other children of this age, again basing their opinions on experience, assume a new baby sibling has been purchased at a store, as have most additions to their environment. In such instances, a correction of a misconception, such as "Babies come from their mothers' bodies," is more helpful than an outpouring of facts, which may simply compound the confusion.

At times parents flood children with information; at other times they protect them with fanciful answers, shielding them from painful realities — "When Aunt Sophie died, she really went to sleep for a long time." That's not true, and it's not helpful. Such a statement may stimulate fantasies and distortions in the child's mind, and contribute to fears about falling asleep. Moreover, such responses evade a primary parental responsibility, which is to prepare a child for the very life realities that the answers are trying to avoid.

Answering questions can be a responsibility. Children think that their parents have all the answers. In the words of one child, children are "whyers" and parents "becausers." Parental fallibility is something that will strike them powerfully when they approach adolescence, as parents of teen-agers know. Obviously, adults can't always be right. But there must be some middle ground between answering questions too fully and confusingly and answering them erroneously, for "the sake of the child."

It is helpful for parents, and for anyone else working with children, to know something about the questions children ask, what the questions mean to the child, and why they ask them. This makes it easier to know what kind of answer is really appropriate, if indeed any answer is required at all. Children's questions are often qualitatively different from those of adults. Some questions aren't even intended to gain information. For the toddler, questions may simply be a test flight, trying out the interrogatory machinery, pulling a lever here, pushing a button there. Ruth Weir, the linguist, preserved one such practice session by tape-recording her 2½-year-old son as he fell asleep alone in his room: "What color blanket? What color hat? What color glass? Not the yellow blanket, the white. It's not black, it's yellow. Where yellow blanket . . . yellow blanket? Yellow light. Where is the light? Here is the light."

Question-and-answer practice takes a more sosphisticated form in the slightly older child, who may answer his own questions as he builds on his immediate experience. "Where do stars come from?" a five-year-old asked as his mother was preoccupied with baking a pie and then using the excess dough. "I know how stars are made," he announced after a few minutes of watching her. "They make them from what's left over from the moon."

Of course a great many questions are intended to gain information and do require an answer. But often they have an

underlying purpose in addition to information gathering.
They may represent a child's attempt to deal with fears or
to gain attention, or they may be a search for security or
reassurance, or an effort at separating the real from the
fantastical.

Questions reflect the predicaments of childhood, and so
allow the reflective parent a view of the growing, struggling
mind. It is important, as we hope to show you, that you try
to answer the whole question, which is more than the words
that express it and which is closely linked to the developmental stage of the child. Think of the question as the start
of a two-way conversation rather than a question-and-answer
session. Sometimes it may be necessary to learn what children think about the subject and what misconceptions they
may have before providing an answer.

In addition, be aware that your own experiences in dealing with difficult topics affect your responses. Your attitude
as you answer a question can convey more to your child than
the words you use.

To give one example — the subject will be dealt with at
length later in the book — the vast majority of children under the age of nine have little comprehension of the finality
of death. But death and loss do have intense meanings to
them. Taking your cue from the child's developmental level,
you might respond to a question about death from a very
young child with a reassuring hug, which confirms your presence and support, rather than with kind words, which have
little meaning to her.

In any event, as important as answering questions is providing an atmosphere that encourages them. As you might
expect, research shows that curious, questioning children are
better equipped emotionally and intellectually than the less
curious. They do better in school, are generally quicker at
solving problems, more flexible, and more creative.

This book developed naturally out of our personal and

professional lives. We've both raised several children and struggled, with varying degrees of success, with their questions. Our mutual interest in the theories of Jean Piaget has resulted in the publication of a book, tapes, and films aimed at making his work more accessible to teachers, psychologists, and others working with children.

In this book we draw on ideas generated by Piaget, Freud, and Margaret Mahler, as well as on the work of many researchers, and we relate their ideas to the concerns of parents. But informing parents on what's new in child-development research is only one part of our goal. The other is to enhance parents' sense of competence in responding to their children's questions.

In addition to our survey of the child-development literature, our material derives from our professional experiences. Ruth Formanek is professor of education at Hofstra University, consulting psychologist at the Jewish Community Services of Long Island, and a psychoanalyst in private practice. Anita Gurian has created educational materials for children and is on the child psychology staff at the Learning Diagnostic Center of Long Island Jewish Hospital–Hillside Medical Center. Over the past sixteen years we have conducted studies and interviews, many of which have appeared in professional journals. Our work has also been enriched by contributions from teachers, students, and parents. Parent groups have helped us establish "listening posts" in preschools and elementary schools.

What we hope to do in this book is provide some insight into what a child's questions mean, with emphasis on some of the really tough ones. Our aim is to help parents match their responses to children's questions by considering their child's developmental level, both emotional and intellectual, as well as some of the meanings hidden behind the question. What's most important is that we hope you'll discover ways of coming up with your own answers.

1

Questions — the Germ of Intellectual Curiosity

LONG BEFORE children can ask questions, almost from the very beginning of life, they're curious. Even without words, they actively explore their surroundings. Some infants are capable of following a red toy with their eyes as early as fifteen minutes after birth. During the first months, infants differentiate among checkerboard, bull's-eye–target, and newspaper-headline patterns, preferring such patterns to plain colors. They show a particular interest in patterns resembling a human face.

As infants begin to move around, first by crawling, then by walking, their explorations into the space around them increase. They also begin to experiment with things: what they can do, what they may be used for, whether they come apart and can be put together again. They fit pots inside each other, put pennies into cups, snap off flowers, listen to differences in sounds, feel differences in weight, smell different fragrances, note that things fall when they let go of them, and look for things that have disappeared.

By the middle of the second year toddlers can walk, run, climb, and get into anything. Until now they have experimented with tangible objects within their reach. Now they're able to imagine things not there, to use one thing to get another, push aside obstacles, anticipate events, solve simple problems. Piaget describes his daughter Jacqueline at one year, eight months, as she arrives at a closed door

> with a blade of grass in each hand. She stretches out her right hand toward the knob but sees that she cannot turn it without letting go of the grass. She puts the grass on the floor, opens the door, picks up the grass again and enters. But when she wants to leave the room things become complicated. She puts the grass on the floor and grasps the doorknob. But then she perceives that in pulling the door toward her she will simultaneously chase away the grass which she placed between the door and the threshold. She therefore picks it up in order to put it outside the door's zone of movement.

Language adds a new dimension to children's explorations. By the age of four, they have learned that things have names, that words can express wishes, ideas, feelings. Preschoolers are the world's most inquisitive creatures, with seemingly tireless minds working constantly to comprehend what's going on. As they become aware that there is a broader and varied environment out there, they seek to explore it, to conquer it. Listen carefully to your child at about 2 to 2½ years, and most likely you'll hear questions, although not in adult form. They're usually straight sentences marked by a rising inflection: "Doggie go away?" "Car broke?" The purpose of such early yes/no questions is to confirm an observation rather than to obtain new information.

In a short time your child will begin to add the "wh" words (*who, what, where, why, when,* and also *how*) to the simple sentence, although the child is still unable to adjust the word order into the question form. Some three-year-olds' questions sound like this: "What the boy hit?" "What she ride?" "Why John can't swim?" Before much longer, they change the word order, add auxiliary verbs, and produce grammatically correct questions: "Why can't John swim?" "What did the boy hit?"

What Does Your Child Want to Know?

Most early questions are about the names of things and places. Each new name becomes an exciting addition to the word collection, and children practice using the name, over and over, at times trying the patience of those around them. Once they get started, they absorb new words in rapid succession.

Frequently you and your child will attach different meanings to words. When children learn a new word, they often use it in a personal, concrete, literal way. Part of understanding their questions is understanding the meaning they give to words. One preschooler searched the neighborhood streets for the "fork in the road." Another became quite distressed when told he had "his father's eyes" and wanted to know how his father would manage without them.

Sometimes the meaning of a word lies in its context. This is especially true of words with a strong emotional charge, such as curses. "Son-of-a-bitch!" exclaimed a three-year-old girl when she hurt her hand. When asked about what she said, she explained that Mommy had said that when she hit her hand with a hammer. The child had generalized from one experience and assumed that the expression properly accompanied hurting one's hand.

Often children don't expect to get answers to their questions, and will provide the answers themselves. Said four-year-old Alice, "What's the snow for? To play in." Nicolai Chukovsky quotes four-year-old Josef, naked in front of a mirror, conducting his own question-and-answer session: "Eyes are for seeing. Ears are for hearing. Mouth is for eating. And bellybutton ... What's it for? Must be for beauty."

Many of the early "why" questions are not requests for information but expressions of surprise or amazement, sometimes of protest. "Why Alice hit me?" "Why I have to go to bed?" However, by about four years information becomes a question's major purpose: "Where is the plane going?" "Is God everybody's father?" "Why are leaves green?"

It is because children believe that everything has a purpose that they ask why stars shine, why rain falls. A scientific answer is beside the point. "To make light" and "to make the ground wet" are answers more meaningful to the child.

Most parents know only too well that the five-year-old asks more complex questions. John Dewey, the philosopher, described this stage of questioning:

> He asks in succession, what holds up the house, what holds up the soil that holds the house, what holds up the earth that holds the soil... but his questions are not a demand for scientific explanations; the motive... is simply eagerness for a larger acquaintance with the mysterious world in which he is placed... In the feeling that the facts which directly meet the senses are not the whole story, that there is more behind them and more to come from them, lies the germ of intellectual curiosity.

Making Connections

Children under five look for links between events, try to make sense of what is happening, but don't always adequately distinguish between the real and the unreal, between the possible and the impossible. They believe that they influence events, that anything that happens has something to do with them. They cannot fathom that some things happen by chance, without anyone's having anything to do with their occurrence. They also assume that inanimate things are similar to themselves, that they can also feel, wish, think, and do. "Is the car too tired to climb up the hill?" "Is the house lonesome when we go away?" "Why did that bad chair hurt my leg?" They may believe that events are related merely because they follow each other in time. This search for connections often leads them to some unusual conclusions:

When 4½-year-old Myra saw her first dramatic sunset she happened to be riding with her parents in a car whose tire had gone flat. For some time afterward, whenever the sky turned red and purple, she would ask, "Are we getting a flat tire?"

Robert was 3½ when his parents took him to see stuffed animals in the museum and explained to him that these animals had once been alive. When he found out that his grandfather had died before he ever knew him, he asked if he could visit him in the museum.

When three-year-old Sue was told her uncle was going to the hospital, she said, "Will he get a baby?"

Piaget's young daughter, seeing the clouds of smoke rising from her father's pipe, assumed that he was responsible for the clouds in the sky and the mists around the mountain tops of Switzerland.

Piaget was fascinated by children's questions. In one of his studies he analyzed 1,125 questions asked by a boy between the ages of six and seven. The boy was encouraged to ask anything he liked and was not aware that his questions were being recorded. Piaget grouped the boy's "why" questions into three types:

1. "Why do things always fall down?" "What makes the train move?" Such questions indicated that the boy was trying to understand physical causes and their effects.

2. "How come Daddy doesn't feel like going to the zoo?" "Why is Robert so mean?" These questions suggested that the boy was trying to understand psychological states, motives, purposes, and moods.

3. "Who said we can't skate on the highway?" "Why do I have to go to school?" These questions indicated that he was

trying to understand the reasons for rules, regulations, and customs.

The "questioning age," the period between three and five, coincides with the period during which sexual curiosity develops, and many questions involve the origin of babies. Many psychoanalysts believe that the positive growth of curiosity and the general desire to learn are derived from the child's early search for sexual information. They believe that curiosity gradually transfers from the sexual to the nonsexual, spreading to interest in such matters as how things work and what other people are like.

According to Freud, all curiosity was originally sexual curiosity. If sexual questions are not answered and if sexual curiosity is discouraged, the child is apt to feel frustrated and interest is not likely to spread to other areas. Moreover, the child's own uncovering of any hidden information may provoke anxiety and prevent the child from developing an interest in further questioning. Young children are unable to figure out why their parents discourage sex-related questions but encourage nonsexual questions. Freud believed that children who are criticized or lied to when they ask about sex may assume they will be similarly treated when they ask about trains, vegetables, or any other topic of interest to them. This idea may seem dated to us now that sexual matters are more openly discussed than they were during Freud's time. However, there are topics in every family that are shut away in the closet, not discussed. Your family, like other families, probably has its share of taboos about particular topics.

Types of Questions

Let's consider what a question may mean to a child. Questions serve many purposes and often come in layers: the question itself and what lies beneath.

The nonverbal question

Questions may be conveyed by means of a gesture, a shrug of the shoulders, a facial expression. A common question of this type is the unspoken "Can you help me?" of the child tugging at her parent's arm. When there is a family crisis, a perplexed or sad facial expression may signal that the child doesn't understand or is fearful but doesn't quite know how to verbalize.

The practice question

Young children in the sheer excitement of acquiring language often repeat a question, at times for the joy of the experience, at other times because they've forgotten the answer, or want the security provided by the repetition, or need time to absorb the information. A child may be looking for an opportunity to display new-found knowledge by turning the question into a game in which she has the fun of answering correctly. She asks, "What color sweater?" and answers herself, "Red!"

The classification question

Preschoolers ask questions to organize their impressions and to make comparisons. A lot of data, fraught with seeming contradictions, have to be sorted out. A table may be red and a block may be red, but clearly a block is not a table. So in one sense they are the same, but in another way they are different. Similarly, one teddy bear may be large and another small, so that although they are the same, they are also different. One way of getting things straight is by asking questions until the discriminations click into place. Sometimes questioning may be a search for confirmation that the name supplied by the parent applies to another similar object. "Bird?" "No, Janie, it flies, but it isn't a bird, it's a kite."

The information question

The school-age child is often seeking straight information, in such questions as "How do computers work?" and "How come the sound and picture on the television come out together?"

The security question

These arise out of children's fears and worries, which often relate to concern about the continued presence of their parents. "Will you be around when I'm big?" "Will you still be my mother when I'm grown up?" "Why can't I go to the movies with you?" Questions such as "Can Godzilla fit through my window?" and "Did King Kong really live?" come as children seek reassurance that there are no monsters, skeletons, ghosts, or creepy-crawly things invading their rooms at night, that the horrors they've witnessed on television remain confined to the screen and are under their control at the flick of a switch.

The pseudo-question

These are questions that don't seek information or reassurance but have some other goal. "Why do I have to go to bed?" is rarely a quest for information but rather an attempt to get some rules changed. The question "Did you know I went to Disneyland?" really communicates, rather than requests, information. "Do you like my new shirt?" is not a question so much as a request for admiration. "Do you want to see me swim?" may represent a wish for an audience to appreciate a new skill. The child is not seeking a verbal yes or no to a question but rather a demonstration of interest in what she's doing or saying, or an exchange of ideas.

The hidden-agenda question

Adults are familiar with the hidden-agenda question. At the end of a long party, the host may ask whether anyone wishes another cup of coffee, a question whose intent may differ from its content — it might really mean, please go home, we're tired and want to go to bed. Very often a child's seemingly straightforward question, such as "What time are you going out tonight?," may have a hidden agenda. The child may hesitate to say straight out that she wishes her parents wouldn't leave her with a baby sitter; by asking for the time, the real intent of the question remains hidden. One way of responding to this question would be to reflect the child's feeling back to her by saying, "I guess you're worried about staying with Suzanne" or "I guess you wish you were going with us." This type of response enables the child to confront her own feelings more directly and to voice them. It's important to bear in mind that the child who constantly asks questions but doesn't listen for answers may be asking for attention rather than for information.

The chained question

This strategy is generally used by older children who may have a goal in mind and will advance it by means of a chain of questions. For example:

SUSAN: Are you really going to marry Bob?
MOTHER: Yes, we'll probably get married in the fall.
SUSAN: I don't like him.
MOTHER: Why don't you give him a chance?
SUSAN: If you get married, will I keep the room I have?
MOTHER: Yes.
SUSAN: Can I paint it any color I like?

As a result of this questioning chain, Susan negotiated self-determination in room painting; but even more than that, she reaffirmed the importance of her place in the family despite the proposed remarriage.

*   *   *

Curiosity, with or without words, contributes to psychological development; children who feel free to explore, to seek new experiences and answers to questions, develop confidence in their own abilities and self-respect. Questions are a means of learning about the world and the people in it. Questions help preschoolers master their environment. For school-age children, questions are critical to learning: they give direction to inquiries; they aid in clearing up confusions and contradictions; they lead to new perceptions and, most important of all, to new questions. Asking the right question is a basic ingredient of creativity.

2

Sex

Where did you come from, baby dear?
Out of the everywhere into the here.

— GEORGE MACDONALD

VERY FEW parents today would include these lines in their children's poetry collection. Parents openly discuss sexual matters with their children more than ever before. Does that mean the children are actually better informed? Research shows that many children are no clearer than they were years ago, despite the emphasis on sex education at home, in school, and in the media.

Lorraine, ten years old: "I got my ideas about babies from 'The Flintstones.' The Rubbles wanted a baby and Betty was crying. A falling star was coming down. She wished, and then the next day on the doorstep was a baby. That's what I thought happened."

Ellen, nine: "I thought you get married, and you wish and you wish and you wish, and if you're good people, then you get a baby."

Parents who faithfully and to the best of their knowledge inform their children about the process of reproduction are often astounded to discover that the children have simplified, mixed up, or elaborated on the facts.

"You go to the store and buy a duck" is the prescription for motherhood of a four-year-old, who was probably told about "the birds and the bees."

"The doctor puts the baby in the mother's tummy and then the doctor takes it out," explained another four-year-old, who evidently was presented with the medical point of view. The medical facts, however, seem to have been merged with his own observations that, when something like a turkey or a chicken comes out of the oven, someone must have put it in.

According to another youngster, "If you want a baby, you buy a body and legs. The mother puts it together and gets the baby." This child seems to use the model-airplane explanation.

Why is it so difficult to communicate ideas about sex and reproduction, even for those who are determined to be open and honest? One reason may be that many of us start in the wrong place. We present the advanced course first, taking for granted certain prerequisites. What are these prerequisites?

Vocabulary

Familiar words acquire new meanings in new contexts. The word *egg* is one of these. An ovum and a chicken egg are obviously not the same; they have different histories and purposes and appearances. But a young child may be confused, because the same word is used for both. The word *seed* is another confusing word. Three-year-old Eric, when told a seed was growing inside his mother, said, "Is there dirt inside her stomach?" When we asked nursery-school children about the word *marriage*, which most of them had heard, their definitions were quite surprising. "It means you kiss and hug a lot," said one. "It means that now your name is Rappaport," said another.

Of course, even if you explain words carefully, you can't

be sure your child will then use them correctly. One mother of a six-year-old had a talk with her daughter about sex, and later heard the child correct one of her friends, "Don't you know the right word for fuck is intercom?"

The idea of gender identity — who is male and who is female

Because children use the words *boy* and *girl* at an early age, you may be fooled into thinking they understand what makes the essential difference. They know someone is called a boy or a girl; pets and dolls are either boys or girls. But what do the words mean to them? Conversations with young children reveal that they know there is a difference between *boy* and *girl* but they're not clear that the critical factor is sexual differentiation. Here are illustrations of some confusions typical in a nursery-school class:

TEACHER: How do you know that your mommy is a girl, Henry?
HENRY: Because she's not a boy.
TEACHER: Debby, how do you know your daddy is a boy?
DEBBY: Daddy is working.
TEACHER: Is that why he's a boy? Doesn't your mommy work?
DEBBY: Yes.
TEACHER: Then is she a boy, too?
DEBBY: No.
TEACHER: How do you know?
DEBBY: She told me.
TEACHER: Lisa, what makes you a girl?
LISA: My mommy wants me to be a girl.

Further questioning revealed that, along with other attributes such as having hair, wearing shoes and socks, playing ball, boys also have a penis and girls a "vagina." But sexual characteristics were not always mentioned as the criteria necessary for making the decision. How does one get to be a boy or a girl? Either parents or God had made the decision. Had they always been either a boy or a girl? Yes. Would they continue to remain whatever they were? On this issue the children were uncertain. Many four-year-olds thought a switch unusual but possible. It was relatively simple — let your hair grow or have your parents or God change their minds. That young children believe almost anything is possible, including a change of gender, fits in with their fascination with fairy tales and other forms of make-believe and sleight of hand.

A sense of time and change

Young children are tuned in to what is present at a particular moment, what is obvious and concrete. Ideas of slow growth, gradual development, and lengthy preparation are hard for them to grasp because they're not within their immediate experience. The development over a long period of time from one form to another (fetus into full-grown baby) is not understood before the age of five or six. Until then children even have trouble with the idea that a person remains the same person despite changes in appearance. In a doctoral dissertation by Sonne Lemke, children were shown photographs of an eight-member family taken several years apart. The youngest children believed that each picture showed different people, because their appearance was different.

The ability to perceive that events have causes

Young children accept what is presented as fact, and it is not until they are five or six that they begin to wonder and to realize that certain events are caused in specific ways. Thus the question "Why do people have babies?" from a very young child may not always be an actual request for a causal explanation.

Understanding what intellectual tools are available to children at different stages and how these affect ideas about sex and reproduction can be a helpful guide to parents. Child psychologists Anne Bernstein and Philip Cowan have done extensive research on children's concepts of how people get babies. They asked children the following questions: "Where do people get babies?" "What does the word *born* mean?" "How do mothers get to be mothers?" "How do fathers get to be fathers?" Not surprisingly, they found that sex information is understood in relation to the child's stage of intellectual development.

The Child Under Five

Most three- and four-year-olds believe that babies have always existed. Since they're concerned with the here and now and don't inquire into causes, these children accept what is directly within their own experience. Some think the mother ate something. Some assume the baby was always in the mother's body. Others think it was somewhere else and then somehow got into the mother's body. These are the responses of one of the children in the Bernstein and Cowan study:

INTERVIEWER: How did the baby happen to be in your mother's tummy?

CHILD: It just grows inside.

INTERVIEWER: How did it get there?

CHILD: It's there all the time. Mommy didn't have to do anything. She waits until she feels it.

INTERVIEWER: You said that the baby wasn't in there when you were there?

CHILD: Yeah, then he was in the other place. In somebody else's tummy.

INTERVIEWER: In somebody else's tummy?

CHILD: Yeah, and then he went through somebody's vagina, then he went in my mommy's tummy.

INTERVIEWER: Whose tummy was he in before?

CHILD: I don't know who his, her name is. It's a her.

At five some children begin to attribute the appearance of babies to a cause and think they come from people who serve as some kind of manufacturers. Laura described it this way: "Maybe they paint the right bones . . . like they get the bones. Then they paint the blood."

"Mommy, Daddy, did you make me?" asked five-year-old Mark. "Yes, we did," said his parents. Mark: "Did you make my jacket, too?"

Five-year-old Michelle attributes the role of manufacturer to God:

INTERVIEWER: How did your mother get Terry?

MICHELLE: God just put a seed in her tummy and she grewed, that's what happened to me and Jennifer. He just put the seed in there and then squished it. I mean, he drilled a hole and squished it in and he put the thing back and then he growed, growed, growed.

INTERVIEWER: Where does he get the seeds from?

MICHELLE: From seeds in watermelon, 'cause when you eat there is pits. You leave them on the table and then God takes them . . . He washes them and dries them off and puts them in Mommy's tummy.

INTERVIEWER: When he put the seed in and the baby grew, how did the baby come out?

MICHELLE: 'Cause she was inside the pit so she grewed out. She wasn't tight enough so it split open, then it was chopped open, and then she grew, grew, grew.

Some children realize that a father may be connected with the process in some way. "He puts his hand in the tummy. Then he puts it on the bottom of the mommy and the mommy gets the egg out of her tummy and puts the egg on top of the seed. And then they close their tummies and the baby is born."

When Michelle, quoted above, was asked if her daddy had anything to do with her sister's birth, she described his contribution: "Yes, she [my mother] had to go to the hospital. She had to have the baby. She had to get there fast. A cop almost catched us, so my daddy told him, 'My wife is having a baby,' so the cop said, 'All right, go fast,' so you could go through red lights, so we did."

It's important to respond to misconceptions. To the child who believes that babies are manufactured, you might say, "That's an interesting way of looking at things. That's the way you'd make a doll. You'd buy a head and some hair and arms and legs and put them all together. But making a real, live baby is different from making a doll or a cake or an airplane." You might tell the child that only people can make other people. To make a baby you need two grown-up people, a man and a woman, to be the baby's mother and father. If questioned further, add that the mother and father make the baby from an egg in the mother's body and a sperm from the father's body.

Five- and Six-Year-Olds

At these ages, children realize that both a father and a mother are involved. According to Michael, "He puts his penis right in the place where the baby comes out and somehow it comes out of there. It seems like magic, sort of, 'cause it just comes out. Sometimes I think the father pushes maybe." John describes conception: "I guess it's like mothers and fathers are related and their loving each other forms a baby. I don't know how it really comes just by loving and stuff. I guess the love forms the beans and I guess the beans hatch the eggs."

Affirm for the child that loving is an important part of having a baby. You might say, "It's really important for a baby that mothers and fathers love each other, so that when the baby is born they can take good care of it. But loving is a feeling and can't start the baby all by itself. A baby is a living person and it starts growing from living people. A sperm from the father goes through his penis into the mother's vagina. When the sperm joins with an egg from the mother, a baby starts growing inside the mother."

Seven- to Nine-Year-Olds

Somewhere between these ages children abandon earlier ideas that rely on magic or manufacture. Ideas about sex at this time generally contain three major ingredients: children recognize that a tie or bond exists between two people, that the mechanics of sexual intercourse take place, and that there is a uniting of biological materials. They recognize all these as part of the process, but are not able to coordinate all of the ideas into a coherent system. These are some children's responses that illustrate how, in a manner that seems logical to them, one idea becomes linked to another:

"When you get married, you go on your honeymoon . . . and you fuck on your honeymoon, you know, and that makes it so you've got each other's germs, and then, when you do it again, you've got a baby. But sometimes you don't do it like for long enough or something and then you don't get a baby."

A seven-year-old boy in one of our studies gave the following account as he integrated information given by his parents in his own personal way. "Well, it's like when people get close together, I mean really close together. Then a sperm comes out of the man through a tiny opening, but they're still really close together that no air can get in. The sperm is like a germ, it swims up a river or a lake or a canal to my mother's womb. But the people just have to get really, really close, and it goes through the tiny holes in the pajamas."

Karen, when asked why the seed and the egg have to come together, replied, "Or else the baby, the egg won't get really hatched very well. The seed makes the egg grow. It's just like plants. If you plant a seed, a flower will grow. It's just a special kind of seed that makes an egg hatch." She had absorbed the information that seed and egg are necessary to create a new life, but she had no clear idea of why this was so.

Even children of nine or ten have trouble understanding why genetic material must unite in order to form a baby. Some believe that the whole baby exists in either the sperm or the egg, needing the other only to touch off the growth.

"I guess when the sperm gets in there it just does something to the egg and it makes it start growing."

Can the egg grow if no sperm goes into it?

"No."

Can sperm grow with no egg?

"No, that doesn't have the baby. It's the egg that would have the baby in it."

Kathy said, "Well, if they're the man that made love to your mother then they're your father because you really originally came out of him and then went into your mother . . . you were a sperm inside of him . . . 'cause he was the one that had you first."

By the age of twelve children have the mental ability to put all the facts together. They give exclusively physical explanations of conception and birth, and realize that both parents contribute the genetic material to the embryo. They are also aware of the moral and social aspects of reproduction. This almost scientifically accurate description of conception was provided by Michael: "The sperm encounter one ovum, and one sperm breaks into the ovum, which produces. The sperm makes like a cell, and the cell separates and divides. And so it's dividing, and the ovum goes through a tube and embeds itself in the wall of the, I think, it's the fetus of the woman."

*   *   *

This guide to development shouldn't be considered applicable to all children everywhere, but only suggests the kind of information a child might be able to understand at a given age. Individual variations are enormous, and children's creativity is boundless, although, with increasing age, their more fantastic explanations become more and more realistic. Remnants of the fantastic, however, may continue to coexist with newer and more accurate information. The earlier fantastic explanations furnish the stuff that dreams, daydreams, stories, and poems are made of.

Merely asking your children what they know about gender, sex, and birth is not by any means a foolproof method of eliciting their thoughts. It's highly likely that many children know more than they can and wish to say. Many children have picked up the message, spoken or unspoken, that sex is a topic evoking particular responses, sometimes evasion or a smile, sometimes embarrassment. Sensitive to adult reaction, children may avoid taking risks with topics that are taboo to some people.

Many of the changes in our attitudes toward raising children derive from the work of Sigmund Freud, who alerted us to the importance of children's sexual questioning. Contrary to the beliefs prevalent in his day, Freud advised parents to enlighten their children on sexual matters, in order to encourage the children's search for all knowledge, not only sexual. He believed that many emotional problems in adult life could be traced to early sexual misunderstandings. According to Freud, certain crucial experiences have the power to stimulate or to block the growth of curiosity, influenced especially by the way parents react to questions. One such important experience is the birth of a sibling. The other is the discovery by the child of his parents in the act of sexual intercourse. According to Freud, children may interpret intercourse as an aggressive act, inflicted by the father on the mother, and both parents may sound as if they were in pain. Others, however, believe that children's reactions depend on their experience with parents generally — whether parents are loving or hostile toward each other — not only on how they behave when they are discovered during the "primal scene."

If a child does happen to come in, an event that is not uncommon, it's not a disaster. If the child doesn't bring it up himself, encourage him to talk about it in order to learn if he has distorted what he has seen and to help him deal with his reactions. Tell him it's an act of love and affection that gives great pleasure, and that it's done in private. Keep it short, simple, and cool.

Learning about sexuality is a process that begins at birth. Sexual feelings and curiosity about sex start long before children can ask questions. The warmth and comfort derived from bathing and sucking are the child's first sensual experiences. She discovers the pleasant feelings to be had from touching and being touched. When the child is a little older, she may discover the pleasure that comes from touching her genitals, a natural and healthy sensation. During the preschool years, children observe one another's bodies, notice similarities and differences. Nursery-school teachers report that the children find it fascinating to watch one another urinate.

At about three or four, often stimulated by the birth of a sister or brother, many children ask questions about birth. Freud, working with the recollections of adult patients, was impressed with the imaginative richness of children's fantasies about the origin of babies: mothers get babies by eating something special; babies come out of the anus, the breast, the belly button, they're cut out of the mother's belly like Little Red Riding Hood out of the wolf.

The time that children begin to ask questions usually coincides with a time of heightened sexual feelings. Freud referred to the stage between four and six years, when the child usually feels a strong attraction to the parent of the opposite sex, as the "oedipal phase," after King Oedipus of Greek mythology, who slew his father and married his mother. Many children openly express a desire to "marry Mommy" or "marry Daddy." We knew a four-year-old girl who started to dig a big hole in the back yard; after several days of digging, she announced the hole's purpose: "It's for Mommy, so I can marry Daddy."

At this age, many children long to exclude the same-sex parent. Parents, however, should not play into their child's fantasies. Here are two possible ways of responding to such longings on the part of a child:

FATHER: My train was late. I'd like to have dinner in a hurry and then relax.
MOTHER: You're not the only one who works hard.
FATHER: I know, I know, but what time are we eating?
MOTHER: Well, dinner was ready an hour ago.
CHILD: I'll warm it up for you, Daddy.
FATHER: I knew I could count on my little sweetheart.
CHILD: Can I make your supper all the time?
FATHER: That would be fine with me. I'm sure you can do as well as your mother.

In this case the father unknowingly responds to his daughter's yearning for him in a way that might encourage her unrealistically. In addition, her mother's abdication may add to a feeling as well as a fear in the child that her wishes might actually come true.

Here's another possible scenario with essentially the same opening line and question on the part of the child:

FATHER: Listen, my train was late and I'm tired. I'd like to have dinner in a hurry and then relax.

MOTHER: Well, our schedule is all off, but if you make the salad we can be ready in a few minutes.

CHILD: Can I help, Daddy?

FATHER: Sure, let's work on the salad together.

CHILD: Can we play we're married and we always make salad together?

FATHER: Well, we can make salad together, but you know I'm married to Mom.

CHILD: Why can't you get a divorce?

FATHER: We want to stay married.

MOTHER: And we want you to be our child.

FATHER: O.K., let's put everything on the table so we can all eat.

In this case the child has been encouraged to express her feelings without anybody getting angry with her, but she has been gently reminded and reassured of her place in the family.

Between the ages of six and ten children expand their world. They gradually resolve the conflicts of the oedipal stage, become more interested in learning about the world and more self-sufficient, and widen their contacts and information through school, friendships, and reading. Although they are ostensibly less interested in sexual matters, there are still many questions and sex play — group trips to the bathroom, hospital and doctor games, and so forth. Masturbation can become a source of anxiety to them. An important factor is your attitude. If you can be calm and accepting, your child will not feel frightened or "bad."

During the preadolescent period, from about nine to thirteen, children's interest in their bodies and in sexuality becomes intensified; they are experiencing many physical changes. Sex hormones are produced, hair grows under the arms and in the pubic area, girls experience the onset of menstruation, the growth of breasts, boys' voices deepen and they have wet dreams. If you've kept the lines of communication open from an earlier day, you will be faced with new questions as the children face problems in regard to moral issues surrounding sex.

General Guidelines

How can we best tell children what they want to know? What will they do with our answers to their questions? Will they accept them as offered? Will they weave them together with their own fantasies, hearsay, and misinformation? It's not an easy job, but the following guidelines may help.

1. Try to find out the meaning of the question to the child. It's important to know the child's own private theories before presenting him with new facts in which he may have no interest. Get the child's ideas first. "Tell me what you think, and then we'll try and figure things out together" is one approach. If your child says something like "The mommy eats something and it comes out through the B.M. place" or "The baby comes out through the mommy's bellybutton," it's important to dispel these misconceptions. Then think about how you can best respond to your child in line with his developmental level, without distorting the truth.

2. Consider the meaning of the question to you. It's important to examine your own feelings about issues related to sex — menstruation, masturbation, intercourse outside of marriage, and other topics. When your child asks, your answer will affect her attitudes and feelings as well as provide facts.

3. Don't tell children more than they want to know. They may take a while to absorb a piece of information and may not comprehend it well enough to ask another question until months later. Wait for their questions. They're sure to come.

4. Many parents feel that by telling their children about

sex they will encourage them to become preoccupied or over-stimulated, and this may lead to experimentation. Don't forget, however, sexual feelings exist even if you don't talk about them, and the children are already receiving a lot of information from other sources — friends, television, movies. Research has shown that children who attended sex-education courses were better able to express and explain their feelings and showed more selectivity in choosing marital partners.

5. Not every sensation and experience can be explained to a child. A recent book on human reproduction designed to be read to children described the sensation of an orgasm by comparing it to a ticklish feeling similar to the one you have when you feel a sneeze coming. Some of us may consider that an inadequate explanation. Can an orgasm be described in words? To a child? What we're saying is, Don't undertake the impossible unless you're a poet.

6. Acquaint yourself with the correct names for the genital organs and use explicit terms with the child. Unless you convey a tone of secrecy, the child will have no more embarrassment with the word *vagina* than with the word *shoulder*. To one mother we know who is a stockbroker, words such as *investment, bonds,* and *interest* came easily, but she used *tummy, wee-wee,* and *dickie* when talking about sex and reproduction with her children.

We quote psychiatrist Richard Robertiello: "By the time she's given birth, a woman will usually have learned the difference between her urethra, vagina, and anus, but there is a split between intellectual grasp and emotional belief. During toilet training she may pass on to her daughter the confusion that these three areas are all lumped together in one idea, "down there" or "your bottom." What has for so long not been expressed in words has obscured the facts about body functions."

7. Talk in terms of human beings. When a child asks about the structure of the body or how babies are made, he's usually thinking about people, and answering in terms

of the birds and bees is evasive and not likely to be applied to human beings.

8. Recognize that sexual feelings are not isolated but are related to many other feelings. The affection that parents display toward each other, toward other adults, and toward their children lays the groundwork for their children's capacity to love.

9. Some children do not ask direct questions, but this does not mean that there are none in their minds. Fantasies and misconceptions may be rife. Be alert to the hidden-agenda question. A child may be showing concern about a woman's prominent middle without being able to frame a direct question. Encouragement from the parent will stimulate a discussion and enable the child to ask her own questions next time.

10. Even families who encourage expressions of curiosity may be at a loss when it comes to handling a common situation, such as finding a young child poring over pornographic magazines, peeking into washrooms, playing "doctor." How parents react to such situations is important. Remaining cool and calm is a help.

11. Research shows that children constantly invent new explanations to account for complex processes. And since their inventions change from week to week, furnishing the "correct" explanation is not quite so important as conveying willingness to discuss the subject. Become an "askable parent," a term coined by Sol Gordon, professor of child and family studies at Syracuse University: "The point is to get across to your child at an early age that you want to be asked questions. If you wait to discuss sex until your child is about to menstruate or have a wet dream, then it's too late to become an askable parent." If you are able to accept your children's questions about sex as evidence of their curiosity about the world about them, it will become just another part of the growing-up process, rather than a mystique that becomes titillating simply because of its secrecy.

Questions Frequently Asked by Children Under Five

The suggested answers consist of short, direct responses that usually supply the information the child is seeking. Those answers marked with an asterisk represent additional responses helpful when the child asks for more information.

Why is that lady so fat?
"There's a baby inside her."
You mean she swallowed a baby?
"No, she didn't swallow it. It's growing inside her."
Will the baby stay in there?
"No, it will come out."
How will the baby get out?
"The baby comes out through a special opening in the mother's body."
    * "It's between the mother's legs."
    * "The opening gets bigger and then the baby comes out."
    * "It's a different opening from the opening for urinating or bowel movements."
How come I don't have a penis/vagina? How come Susan doesn't have a penis?
"Boys and girls are different. A boy has a penis and a girl has a vagina."
Why does a penis go up and down?
"That's the way penises are."
Why do women have breasts?
"The breasts can make milk for her baby to drink."
Then why does Johnnie drink from a bottle?
"Some mothers give the baby milk from their breasts and some mothers give the babies milk from a bottle." (One four-year-old thought that nursing made the baby fatter and the mother thinner, probably on the basis of her observation that if you pour something out, it's now in a different place.)

What's a bellybutton for?

"The baby is attached to his mother by a tube. When the baby comes out of his mother he doesn't need the tube anymore. The bellybutton is the spot where the tube was. Navel is another word for bellybutton."

* "The baby gets her food from the tube that connects to her mother, and when she's born she can be fed through her mouth, so she doesn't need the tube."

Can I see your penis/vagina? Can I see the place where I came out?

"I know you'd like to see what a grown-up penis (or vagina) looks like, but I'd rather not show you. I like to have privacy and I know you do, too, sometimes. I'll tell you what you want to know."

* "Let's look at the pictures in this book, which show us what all the parts of the body look like."

There is a difference of opinion on this issue among child therapists. Many feel it is healthy for children below the age of ten or eleven to occasionally see their parents in the nude, in a natural situation, such as showering or changing clothes. This attitude is based on the premise that hiding one's body encourages undue curiosity and secret fantasies. Mio Fredland, assistant professor of psychiatry at Cornell University, states: "My four-year-old daughter loves to look at her vagina. Sometimes when I'm getting out of the shower, she'll come and lie down on my bathroom rug and just stare up at me and say, 'I'd like to see what your vagina looks like and what your rectum looks like,' and I say, 'O.K., have a good look.' "

Find the attitude that suits you best. Child therapists all agree that going out of your way to be nude in front of children is not a good idea.

Where do babies come from?

"A special place inside the mother."

How does the baby get inside the mother?

"Every woman has tiny eggs inside her. They're not the

same kind of eggs we're used to eating. These eggs are very, very tiny, so tiny that they're even smaller than the smallest pencil dot that you can think of. One of those eggs starts to grow in a special place inside the mother. It grows into a baby."

It's not a good idea to use the word *stomach*. Since many children acquire the notion that the only way something can get into the body is by swallowing, misconceptions about eating and having babies may arise.

What's the special place?
"It's called a uterus."

Where is it?
"It's way inside."

Why?
"It's inside to keep the baby warm and protected."

Will a baby grow in me?
"Not now. You're too young. When you grow up a baby will be able to grow in you."

Why can't men have babies?
"Their bodies aren't built for having babies. They don't have a uterus and a vagina. But men certainly do have an important part in making babies. The man's sperm and the woman's egg have to join to make a baby. But only grown-up women have babies and become mothers."

How will I know who to marry?
"When you grow up and fall in love, you will think about whether you will want to marry that person."

Do you make babies out of bones?
"No, only people can make babies. You need two grown-up people to be the baby's mother and father."

Do mothers grow the girls and fathers grow the boys?
"No, all babies grow inside their mother, whether they're boys or girls."

When I was born did you find out I was Jason?
"When you were born we chose the name Jason for you."

Was I inside you?
"Yes."

Was my teddy inside too?
"No."

Questions Frequently Asked by Children Age Five to Nine

Children at these ages have better notions of time, cause and effect, and social relationships, and are ready for more detailed information about the body, pregnancy, birth, and the role of the father. Some of the same questions asked at a younger age will recur, but this time around answers should be more detailed and precise.

How does a baby get inside the mother?
"When a woman wants to have a baby, one of the little eggs inside her starts to grow in a special place called a uterus. Then the baby needs to grow inside the mother for a long time before it's ready to be born."

How do the eggs get inside?
"Every woman is born with the eggs inside her."

How come the egg starts growing?
"A sperm from the father's body joins with the egg inside the mother and the baby starts growing."

How does the sperm join with the egg? Does it hurt when the sperm hits the egg?
"The man's body fits with the woman's body. The man's penis makes the sperm, and the father puts his penis near the entrance to the uterus so the sperm can join with the egg. A fluid called semen comes out of the penis and carries many sperms into the uterus. One sperm joins an egg. This joining

starts the baby growing. You don't actually feel it when the sperm hits the egg."

How do you do sexual intercourse?

"The mother and the father lie close together and feel loving toward each other. The father's penis fits into the mother's vagina. That's called sexual intercourse." (Children at these ages cannot understand the idea of pleasure in intercourse. The process sounds odd to them. They need to be reassured that it is a pleasurable, not a hurtful experience.)

Does the man urinate inside the woman?

"No. Even though the penis does carry the man's urine and semen out of his body, it can't do both at the same time."

* "There's a valve inside the penis, and it automatically shuts off the urine when a man is having sexual intercourse."

Does it hurt when the baby comes out?

"The uterus is a muscle that pushes the baby out. The vagina stretches when the baby comes out. The pushing sometimes hurts, but there's medicine that can help that. Some mothers do special exercises so that the pushing won't hurt."

How do you know when the baby will come out?

"Babies need about nine months to grow inside the mother. You never know the exact day the baby will be born. It can be born a few days or weeks before the nine months are up, or a few days or weeks after the nine months are up."

How come the baby gets bigger inside the mother? How does it eat?

"The baby grows and gets its food from the mother. There's a special cord called the umbilical cord that connects the baby and the mother. The baby gets its food and air through the cord from its mother."

* "The blood vessels of the baby and the blood vessels of the mother are alongside each other, and the food and air pass from the mother's bloodstream into the baby's bloodstream. While the baby is in the uterus, it's curled up inside a bag of fluid called a water bag. This keeps the baby comfortable and safe from being hurt."

Can't the baby drown in the water?
"No, because the baby doesn't breathe the way we do. It doesn't use its lungs until it's born."

Does the baby move around?
"Not at first, but after four or five months it moves its arms and kicks its feet and turns around."

Does it hurt when the baby kicks?
"No, the baby is small, and the kicks are gentle."

How big is the uterus?
"It's about the size of a small pear. It's shaped something like an upside-down pear."

How can a whole baby fit into a pear size?
"It can fit because the uterus stretches as the baby grows. It can stretch up to about twenty times its regular size."

How do you know when a baby is growing inside?
"One way is to have a doctor examine you."
* "A woman usually knows she's pregnant because her menstrual period stops."

Why do you go to the hospital to have a baby?
"Not everybody does. Having a baby is a natural thing and you don't really need a hospital. But most women go because the doctors and nurses are prepared to help them give birth in an absolutely clean place. And then after the baby is born, both the mother and baby get good care, and the mother gets a chance to rest."

How long does it take for a baby to be born?
"Most of the time it takes a few hours. Sometimes only a few minutes, and once in a great while it can take as long as a day."

How do you know when the baby is ready to be born?
"You can usually tell when you feel something like a

cramp or a muscle tightening up. Then the feeling starts to come regularly as the uterus tries to push the baby out. That's what's called labor pains."

* "Another sign can be water coming out. That means the water bag that has protected the baby has broken, and the baby is ready to come out."

What if the baby starts to come out before the mother can get to the hospital?

"Usually the mother feels the cramps in plenty of time. But once a baby starts, nothing can hold it back. Lots of babies have been born at home, or in a taxi or a car, and they're just fine. Even police officers and fire fighters have been trained to deliver babies for mothers who can't get to the hospital on time."

Can a woman have a baby if she's not married? (Children at these ages may have begun to realize that a pregnancy is not always a welcome event.)

"Yes. But sometimes when a woman who isn't married learns that she's pregnant, she isn't very happy. For a long time we've believed that children need a mother and a father and a family. But people nowadays don't get as upset about it as they used to. People in the family and friends help out."

Do you make a baby every time you have intercourse?

"No, the sperm doesn't always join with the egg."

What part of the body has the eggs?

"The eggs are in the ovaries. A woman has two ovaries. They're quite small, about the size of an almond. They're connected to the uterus by a tube."

Does the sperm look like the egg?

"No, it's much smaller than the egg. A sperm looks like a little tadpole with a long tail. It needs a tail because it actually swims to meet the egg."

Does it swim in water?

"No, it swims in a fluid called semen. Semen is made in the testicles, just behind the penis."

Where do the egg and the sperm cell get together?

"In a tube right near the uterus. It's called the Fallopian tube."

Is that where the baby grows? In the tube?

"No, the egg travels down the tube into the uterus and then it begins to grow into a baby."

Can an egg become a baby all by itself?

"No, an egg has to join with a sperm. It's called fertilization when that happens."

Do women always have milk in their breasts?

"No, only after the baby is born and as long as they continue to nurse the baby. If they don't nurse the baby, the milk dries up."

At what age can girls get pregnant? At what age do boys have sperm?

"A girl can become pregnant once her menstrual periods begin if she has intercourse with a boy whose body has begun to make sperm cells. A boy's body starts to have sperm about age twelve."

Can everybody have a baby? Why do some people adopt babies?

"Everybody's body is not exactly the same. There are some men whose bodies make very few sperms, so that there's less chance that the egg inside the woman will be joined by a sperm and start a baby growing. Sometimes a woman doesn't have eggs. Nobody really knows the reasons why. So when a man and a woman have intercourse and they can't start a baby growing and they want to have a child in their family, they may decide to adopt a baby. Sometimes people can have their own children but they want to adopt a baby anyway. They may want to help a child who doesn't have parents, or they may want to have an older child, or they may have some other reason."

Questions Frequently Asked by Children Age Ten to Twelve

Children of these ages are apt to be concerned about bodily changes. Many are scared and some wonder if what's happening to them is normal. Secondary sex characteristics are developing. Breasts are enlarging; voices are deepening; pubic hair is growing. Children need to be reassured that these changes are normal, and since they're watching each other very carefully, they need to know that all bodies are different: they come in various shapes and mature at different rates. All girls will develop breasts, some larger, some smaller. Boys' penises differ in size, as do other organs of the body. Fantasies and questions are stirred up around thoughts of marriage, pregnancy, and birth. It's important to convey facts, but remember, along with each fact you're also conveying your values and attitudes about issues such as dating, premarital sex, divorce, adoption, and roles of family members. In order to open up discussion of these issues, you might consider answering your child's questions with some questions of your own:

Do you think it would be easy or hard for a woman to take care of a baby if she isn't married? Would she need help? What special problems would she have? How could she solve some of these problems? When mothers and fathers work outside the home, what are some of the ways they might arrange for care of their baby? Does a child need two parents?

Sex educators feel that by the age of nine children, especially girls, should be learning about menstruation. In a study conducted by the Project on Human Sexual Development of Cambridge, Massachusetts, it was found that almost 40 percent of the parents of girls aged nine to eleven had never even mentioned menstruation.

Dr. Joae Graham Selzer, in her book *When Children Ask*

About Sex, gives helpful suggestions on how to convey information about menstruation in a way that is both informative and anxiety-allaying. She advises that we begin by telling about the functions of the uterus, Fallopian tubes, ovaries, and vagina. If you can sketch, a diagram can be enormously helpful. If your sketching is inadequate, find a diagram in a book.

Questions about menstruation

When will I menstruate?

"Girls get their first menstrual period at different ages. You may get your first period when you're ten, or you may get it when you're twelve or thirteen."

What happens when you menstruate?

"You have two ovaries with hundreds of little, tiny eggs in each of them. Each month one of those tiny eggs becomes ripe. It gets larger and leaves the ovary. It goes into the Fallopian tube near the ovary. The egg is called an ovum. One month one ovary produces a ripe ovum and the next month the other ovary produces a ripe ovum. The ovum passes down the tube into the uterus. This takes a few days to happen."

Why does a menstrual period happen?

"Each month the uterus gets ready in case a baby will grow in it. Girls don't have babies at ten or eleven. They're not ready to take care of a baby, but the uterus starts to get ready."

How does the uterus get ready?

"The lining of the uterus gets thicker. A kind of cushion is made that would protect a baby. But if a sperm cell doesn't join the egg cell you don't need this cushiony lining in your uterus. The tiny egg and the extra lining come out of the uterus and out of the vagina. That's what's in the menstrual blood. For some people this can take a couple of days. For others it can take about a week. Menstrual blood is clean, and it doesn't mean that anything inside of you is hurt or damaged."

But what if it doesn't stop? What if I go on bleeding?

"Menstrual blood almost always stops. In the very rare case when it doesn't, we should go see a doctor."

What do you do about the blood coming out? What if it pours out?

"It doesn't just pour out. It drips out. You have to wear something to soak up the blood, so it doesn't get you wet and stain your clothes. Some women wear cotton pads." (It's reassuring to show different kinds of pads, belts, and tampons. Practical questions as to what to do if it starts in school and whether it hurts should be encouraged.)

Can you urinate when you're having a menstrual period?

"Yes. Remember, the menstrual blood comes out of your vagina. When you urinate, the urine comes out of a different opening, called the urethra. The menstrual blood has nothing to do with urinating or having a bowel movement."

Do you have menstrual periods forever?

"No. Menstrual periods usually stop about the time a woman is fifty years old. Then she can't become pregnant anymore."

Questions about erections and wet dreams

Why does a penis go up and down? Is there a bone inside?

"It happens naturally; there's no bone inside. A penis has many vessels that fill up with blood, and then the penis gets stiff and hard. That's called an erection. Usually men get erections with sexual excitement, but it can be caused by other things, too, such as having to urinate or being cold or being very frightened. It happens to all boys and men."

What happens when a boy has an erection?

"Sometimes it just disappears. Sometimes semen comes out of the penis. That's a white, sticky fluid. When the semen comes out, it's called an ejaculation, and the person feels an extra-special pleasure that makes him feel relaxed and good all over. That's called an orgasm. It can happen when he's masturbating or having intercourse or even when he's dreaming. That's what we mean by a wet dream."

How often do boys have wet dreams?

"It's different for everyone. Some have them a few times a week; some boys have them a few times a year; and some aren't aware of having them."

Where does the semen come from?

"The semen is made in the testes. When a boy reaches the age of about twelve or thirteen, sperm are made inside the testes, and they're carried in the semen."

If sperm come out during a wet dream will there be any left?

"The testes make sperm all the time and they continue doing it for a man's whole life."

Why does hair grow under your arms and between your legs?

"Early cave men and women were covered with hair all over their bodies. It kept them warm and protected. As far as we know, hair in these two parts of the body still may serve as some kind of protection."

Questions about pregnancy and intercourse

How old does a girl have to be to become pregnant?

"Soon after her menstrual periods begin she can become pregnant if she has sexual intercourse."

How can you tell if you're pregnant?

"If a woman has sexual intercourse and then she has no menstrual periods for a few months, she may be pregnant. Since menstrual periods sometimes don't come on time every month, you can use tests to make sure."

If you have intercourse when you're pregnant, can you become pregnant again?

"No. When a woman is pregnant her ovaries don't discharge eggs, so she can't become pregnant."

Why do people have sexual intercourse?

"It's very enjoyable and it's a natural thing to do."

How did the first people on earth know what they had to do to have intercourse?

"It seems to be a natural instinct. Sexual intercourse is the way a species reproduces itself. Otherwise, human beings would become extinct."

What do you do when you want to have a baby?

"A man's body is made to fit with a woman's body so that sperm have a way of getting to the egg. The reason a woman's reproductive organs are inside her body is so that the baby can be kept warm and safe. The man's penis gets hard and fits into the woman's vagina. The sperm come out of his penis and swim up into the uterus and meet the egg. One sperm combines with the egg and then the egg divides into two halves, and then four parts, and more, and pretty soon it begins to grow into a baby."

What happens to the other sperm?

"They just disintegrate."

How do you know when it's over?

"After the man has had an ejaculation and the sperm has come out of his penis, the penis isn't hard anymore and intercourse isn't possible for a while. The man and the woman feel pleasure and loving and warm toward each other."

What if a man and woman want to have intercourse but they don't want to have a baby?

"There are ways of preventing the egg cell and the sperm cell from joining. This is called birth control."

Does birth control always work?

"Most of the time it works. If it doesn't and the woman becomes pregnant, she can decide to have an abortion. That means that the doctor takes out the fertilized egg."

How old should a person be when they start to have intercourse?

"They should be old enough to understand what it's about and be willing to accept the results."

Other questions of concern to children

Kids say you're a faggot if you like boys and you're a boy. Is it bad to like boys if you're a boy?

This is a question to be answered in accordance with your own values. Anne Bernstein, who has done considerable research into the sexual attitudes of children, points out that same-sex friendships and crushes are a natural part of growing up. She feels the important issue is to point out the value of such friendships and to help the child avoid conflicts about them. She recommends that parents explain both homosexuality and heterosexuality and admit their prejudices to their children. If they disapprove of homosexuality, explicitness about social values will give their children important information. "The world is like that." Some parents may wish to emphasize that each person's choice should be respected and derogatory terms should not be used.

How old do you have to be to masturbate?

This question, posed by a ten-year-old, alerts us to the sharp change that has taken place in recent years about masturbation. Old fears that masturbation was unhealthy and could cause any number of ailments, from warts on the hands to softening of the brain, are simply not true. The most common ill effect of masturbation is the one caused by horrified and punitive reactions to it, which make the child feel it's a bad, dirty habit. Recent sex research suggests that masturbation is prerequisite to adult sex. Masturbation is a form of learning about one's body, how it works, what it's like. To the young child who wants to know why his parents frown on masturbation in public, you might say "I know it feels good and it's all right, but it makes me uncomfortable when you do it in public, and I would feel better if you'd go to your room, where you can have privacy." Or, "It's something you do in private."

It's important to convey to the child that it's perfectly normal. Most of us have to deal with our old conflicts about it. By this time you're probably getting anxious, so we hasten to assure you that it is indeed a tough job. William Block, author of *What Your Child Really Wants to Know About Sex and Why*, suggests that to the child of nine or ten you might say something like:

> "I know you masturbate. It's not harmful...and if it ever troubles you, come to me and we'll talk about it." It's pretty hard to bring the word up for the first time in a casual way. But try and drop it into the conversation; with a movie you saw, a book you read, or you may have heard a joke that you'd rather not repeat because it speaks of masturbation as a crummy, gross or disgusting habit when you know it to be an acceptable part of growing up. And you might even add, "I wish someone had told me that when I was a kid. It took me ten years to get over being guilty about something my doctor told me was as normal to growing up as smoking cigarettes behind the barn."

3

Divorce

"WHEN ARE YOU and Daddy getting divorced?," five-year-old Roy asked his happily married parents. His assumption that divorce is the automatic sequel to marriage makes sense in light of current statistics. A study conducted in 1976 found that there were twenty million American children under eighteen whose parents were separated. Twenty million children can ask a lot of questions!

At one time it was taken for granted that a marriage, no matter how miserable, should be preserved for the sake of the children. The belief more prevalent today is that a tension-filled two-parent home can be more stressful for a child than a peaceful one-parent home. Other taken-for-granted notions are also being challenged. It's no longer automatically assumed that the mother will have custody of the children. Families are working out a variety of arrangements: a father may retain custody (the 1976 study showed that close to one million children of divorced parents lived with their fathers); custody may be shared; some parents even seem to be able to live in separate apartments in the same building in order always to be accessible to their children.

Children of divorce ask the same questions as other children, plus some others unique to their life situation. Unique to the situation also is the fact that divorced parents are often in a particular state of confusion and upheaval. Divorce can create hurts and hostilities that unleash furies people didn't know resided within them. Talking to a child has a low priority when you're quivering with anger, incensed at some outrageous allegation, or just depressed — all common states for a person undergoing or contemplating a divorce. Calm, rational responses aren't always possible, or even appropriate or desirable. Parents, embroiled in their own conflicts, often find it difficult to respond to their children's basic needs, let alone to their questions.

One distraught father left home abruptly with the words "Kids, I'll see you next Saturday." His puzzled younger son said, "What's different about that?" The older boy said, "Won't we see you on the other days?" The father then acknowledged that they wouldn't. He did not, however, discuss his divorce plans with his children. What he did transmit to them, along with the information that he was leaving, was that discussion would not be welcome.

Lack of information, however, doesn't stop children from wondering what's going on. Aretha, aged nine, said, "One morning I woke up and my father was gone. I found out by listening to my mother talking to my grandmother on the telephone that he was living downtown. I asked my mother what was happening. She cried, but she wouldn't tell me."

In a long-range, ongoing study called The Children of Divorce Project, started in 1971 in California, Judith Wallerstein and Joan Kelly interviewed children between the ages of 2½ and 18 in an attempt to assess the effects of divorce. They found that most of the preschoolers in their study had been given no explanations at all for their parents' divorce. A parent simply vanished, and they had no idea what had happened.

The counselors in the project, attempting to encourage the children to ask questions and to talk about the divorce, developed what they called their "divorce monologue," which goes something like: "Maybe I could tell you how other children feel when their parents get a divorce. Sometimes they're very worried and they get frightened. They don't understand what happened, and they're scared to ask. They're afraid that asking will upset their mother. They've seen her cry, and they don't want to make her cry again. Sometimes there are fights in the house, and that's very scary, so they just feel very sad, mixed-up, angry feeling . . ." They found that, even among the youngest children, those who were specifically told that one of their parents was going to live somewhere else were less distraught than those whose parent had simply disappeared with no explanation.

Most therapists agree that children who can voice their questions and count on reasonable responses are in a better position to deal with the grief, the confusion, and the anger. Richard Gardner, author of *Psychotherapy with Children of Divorce,* states, ". . . considering the healthy purposes of the grief reaction, I would consider it pathological if a child who is old enough to appreciate what is happening did not react with grief."

Some General Guidelines
Whether to tell

You have to. "It's hard for kids to understand. I hang on to the idea that he'll understand later on. If we can just keep our balance, stay on an even keel for a while, then he'll be able to look at things from a more mature viewpoint and understand," said one mother explaining her reasons for not discussing her divorce with her son. But you can't assume that if the child doesn't ask questions he's unaware of what's happening. If you listen, you're sure to spot a hidden-agenda question. It may take the form of asking about what the neighbors are fighting about, requests for the whole family to do things together, a preoccupation with a television program depicting a separated family, and so on.

You should specifically explain that you're getting a divorce. Some children will not be surprised; they've heard fights and perhaps talk about separation before. To others the news will come as a surprise. Possibly they've been protected by their parents from hearing arguments; perhaps the family style is to keep disagreements unvoiced. Some children whose parents fight continuously may think fighting is a normal procedure and then are shocked to hear about a divorce. Alfred, ten: "My parents used to fight all the time. I used to watch programs like 'I Love Lucy' and they were always fighting. I thought that's what being married was: you marry somebody and you fight. There was one show, 'The Mothers-in-Law,' and they got along all the time. I really didn't understand it."

In most cases there have been clues of separation. A husband may have left for a motel or another apartment; a wife may have taken the children to her parents or a friend's home. Usually there have been a few trial runs.

One mother, reluctant to tell her five-year-old about the separation, informed him that his father had taken a job in Florida. The child constantly asked when his father would be home. When he did not appear, the boy assumed he was dead. The mother, with only the best intentions, allowed this misconception to persist. When suddenly one day the father appeared, the child was overwhelmed and, needless to say, quite shocked.

Who should tell

Most experts agree that if at all possible the news of the divorce should be shared by all the children and both parents together. This helps the children feel a sense of unity and openness with one another; by contrast, if each child is told separately the others may wonder if secrets are being kept. In an open atmosphere the children experience the fact that both parents are available for discussion and are planning for the children even though the parents themselves may be in conflict. After the initial discussion there will probably be many other discussions, which may take different forms: some children want to talk to each parent separately; children of different ages require different levels of information.

Some parents feel that in talking to their children they will not be able to control their emotions — they may cry. Don't forget, the children will be aware of your distress, whether you like it or not. Allow yourself to cry. If you do, your children will know that it is permissible for them to express their sadness by crying also.

Many parents find it impossible to cooperate in telling the children. If this is so, one parent should try to tell the children at a time when he or she is reasonably free from anger toward the other. This time may never occur for some people, but think of it in comparative terms; even the most volatile situation has periods of relative calm.

When to tell

If possible, tell the children while you're still living together as a family. If both parents remain available for talk and questions, the children will have time to get accustomed to the idea. Remember, however, that too long a waiting period before the separation may prolong the agony and enable the child to deny the facts. Also, younger children cannot estimate or judge time. If you haven't made a final decision, postpone telling the children until you're certain. Ups and downs are tough on them.

What to tell

The truth. You really have no choice, since the children will have made their own observations. They usually know, anyway. If they've heard or witnessed bitter arguments, there has to be an open acknowledgment of the fact that there are serious disagreements; it simply isn't possible to have fights and make believe that everything is sweetness and light in front of the children. Telling them there's nothing wrong will force them to doubt their own judgments, and deception or evasion may lead the children to brood excessively over such unvoiced questions as Why don't they tell the truth? Are they hiding something? Am I hearing wrong? What's really going on? Do they think I'm dumb? When, however, children's impressions are validated by their parents, they learn to trust their own perceptions and to trust their parents. It's better to tell the children than to let them guess.

Some parents have found it helpful to ask the children directly what they think about the separation. Although the typical reaction is shock, dismay, or tears, some children actually express relief. One six-year-old said, "Does that mean there won't be any more fights?" One philosophical older child said, "Well, if it's going to be going on like this, it's not good to be together." "Why did it take you so long to decide?" asked one teen-ager. In specifically asking the children in these cases for their reactions, they were encouraged first to identify their feelings for themselves and then to verbalize them. Just as important, the stage was set. They knew they weren't shut out: their opinions mattered and their questions would be honored. This doesn't mean, however, that it's a good idea to ask the children if they think their parents should separate. This is a responsibility that belongs to the parents.

Gilbert Kliman, director of the Center for Preventive

Psychiatry, in White Plains, N.Y., states that the parents should let the child know as soon as possible what the expected reality will be. Obviously, what you tell will depend on the age of your child, how much he or she already knows, and what the relationship is to each parent.

How to tell

Of great importance is how parents communicate their perceptions of each other to their child. If one parent continually runs the other down, the child may feel the need to align with one against the other. As nine-year-old Will said, "You never know which side to go on. If your father says something, you don't know if he's right or if your mother's right. Things go back and forth. It's like a seesaw, and you're stuck in the middle." A loyalty conflict can arise, resulting in guilt feelings and an inability on the part of the child to identify in a loving way with a parent. When one parent is verbally degraded or vilified by the other, the child is apt to feel herself degraded also.

On the other hand, a falsely positive, unrealistic picture will mislead the child. Pretended amicability can be carried too far; it then sets the child to wondering how come his parents are separating if everybody is so loving and friendly. Children can tolerate expressions of heated emotions; what's hard to tolerate is uncertainty.

Another pitfall to be avoided, if at all possible, is going into excessive and intimate detail. This places a burden on the child. "How do you think I feel when your father goes out every night?," "That's some mother you have — she's always running around," "If your father would take a bath once in a while I wouldn't mind getting into bed with him," "Your mother lied about where she was yesterday," are remarks that cast children in the role of confidant and alter their position as children. Forcing them into an adult role may confuse them.

If children ask questions about intimate and personal details that you don't feel it appropriate to share with them, don't evade the questions. Let them know you're not going to answer those specific questions, as well as why. In this way they won't get the idea that all questions are out-of-bounds. You might say, "We want you to ask all the questions that come to mind. I'm sure we'll answer most of them the best we can. But there are some things that we feel are personal and private, and we don't feel comfortable discussing them with you. I'm sure you, too, have private thoughts sometimes you don't want to share with us."

If you can acknowledge your own feelings of confusion, anger, disappointment, rejection, your child will be freer to experience and to admit to similar feelings. While the words you use will vary according to your individual situation, the atmosphere that you establish will convey your real feelings more dramatically than words.

After you tell

Expect some fallout. Distress and anxiety are inevitable and can take many forms — tears, silence, open anger, and indirect signs such as physical illness or a return to earlier ways of behaving.

Cindy, eight: "It really came as a surprise to me. I really couldn't believe it. I stood there and just looked at them. Then something kind of whacked me out of it and I just started screaming and howling the minute I got into my own bedroom."

Priscilla, twelve: "At first I couldn't believe it. I ran to my room and I pinned a letter on my door. It said, 'If you love me, how can you do this to me?' Then my brother talked to me and made me realize that for us to be happy they have to be happy, too."

Some children deny that they are in any way affected.

John, nine: "I don't really think about my father. I just

do schoolwork, watch TV, read some books. I don't really care about him. You can't do much about divorce."

For some children, the initial unhappiness will subside in a relatively short time. Parents report:

"My kids are doing better than I am. I really dreaded telling them, and it was awful at first. But they seemed to bounce back and we got settled."

"I was really afraid my middle daughter would crack. She was always such a sensitive child. But it didn't take too long. At first she didn't want to go to school, because of the other kids, but after a while she became interested in her own goings-on. She really surprised me."

Some children's reactions on the positive side:

Katie, thirteen: "I like it better when they're separated. I see my father on weekends when he's in town. That's more fun 'cause when they were living together I didn't have any time with my father at all."

Daniel, eleven: "It's a big adjustment. You have to learn how to go on with life even with all these changes. No, I don't mind it. As a matter of fact, I'm really happy. I'm not happy because my parents didn't get along but I'm happy now because they're happier. My father and I have a very close relationship, and if there's ever something bothering me, I can always go to my father or my mother. It's not like I don't have somebody to go to just because they're divorced."

Patty, twelve: "I know what they did is right. My father has changed a lot and so has my mother. I don't think that together it would work. They've changed for the better."

Alice, nine: "My father is always nearby. If I want him or need him I can always go over there. I don't think I love either one of them more than I did before they got divorced."

But some other children may have long-lasting negative reactions. According to their parents:

"Charles was always bumping into things and falling. He never did that before. Then it got so he didn't want to go out of the house."

"Lisa seems to tune out a lot. Her teacher says she day-dreams most of the time. She seems just about to cry, but she never does."

According to children:

Natalie, six: "Sometimes when my father leaves me at my house, I look out the window and I wave to him and sometimes I start to cry."

Ten-year-old Wallace felt guilty: "To tell you the truth, I'm upset about my parents' divorce. I think that they would have enough sense because they're grownups, that they wouldn't argue. The reason they got divorced was my father wasn't giving my mother enough money to pay for me and my things. Sometimes I think that it was my fault, because I was born and they have to pay for me. They just couldn't put up with it anymore. So they got divorced. Sometimes I think that I caused it and sometimes I don't."

Cindy, ten: "Sometimes when I look at a picture of my mother holding me and my father with his arms around her, I feel like I wish that he was still here living with us and I cry."

Anger is a common reaction. It can be expressed openly: "I won't go with either one of them! I'm furious with them!" one eleven-year-old stated vehemently. Bart, seven, said, "I wanted to punch them out!" Or it can take more subtle forms, such as stubbornness, lack of cooperation, even a refusal to see one or both parents.

Wallerstein and Kelly in the Children of Divorce Project found that most children, irrespective of age, are at first upset by their parents' separation, but by the end of a year more than half make a good adjustment and return to normal development.

Of course, when reactions become prolonged and are disabling to the child, look for individual professional help.

*   *   *

It's natural for children to wonder and to worry and to ask a lot of questions as they try to cope with and make sense out of a new set of circumstances. Changes are threatening. Some children, even after witnessing bitter parental battles, would still prefer that their parents stay together.

Try to respond in a way that lets the children know the door is open. "You're too young to understand" and "I can't talk about it now" are door-slammers. Curiosity, however, is not thus shut out; it merely goes underground. Lack of explanations may lead to fantasy and to distorted ideas of what is actually taking place. Although children's repetitious questioning may become trying, they seem to need the repetition in order to come to terms with the new state of affairs and their feelings about it.

What are the particular concerns and questions likely to arise in the minds of children of divorce? How can you gauge what questions mean at different ages? We'll deal mainly with two age periods — the preschool years (up to five) and middle childhood (six to twelve) — and discuss what children are capable of understanding at each period and what their emotional needs are. Both intellectual level and emotional needs affect their capacity to deal with the divorce experience.

The Preschool Child

Preschoolers do not always distinguish between reality and fantasy, what they imagine and what actually exists. If they wish for something to happen and then it does occur, they may believe they have caused the event. Because one event follows another, they assume there's a connection between the two. If the parents separate after a child has misbehaved, she may think she's responsible.

Sally, now ten, remembers: "A couple of times I thought that I did it [caused the divorce] because of the times that day

I was bad. I thought they must be fighting because of me."
Young children cannot understand other people's motivations or feelings. If their parents quarrel, they think it must be about them, for it's hard for them to conceive that parents can argue about things or people other than themselves. They may interpret the quarreling as punishment for something they have done wrong, or even thought wrong — they don't clearly separate thought and action; thought equals action in their magical world (I hate him; he disappears; I caused it). It's important to emphasize again and again to children that merely thinking something cannot make it happen. Help them sort out the real from the imagined.

Many preschoolers, believing that their parents are perfect, omnipotent, and incapable of wrongdoing, are convinced that the divorce must therefore be their, the preschoolers', fault. "If I'm good, will Daddy come back?," "Is Mommy mad because I broke the lamp?," "Are you getting a divorce because I watch television when you go out?" are questions frequently asked by children fearful that they have caused the separation.

Be aware that preschoolers think and talk in concrete, literal terms. When they hear a phrase such as "losing your temper," they may wonder where the lost temper can be found. Similarly, other expressions they may hear in times of crisis — raising your voice, crying your eyes out, going to pieces, falling apart, picking on each other, you follow in your father's footsteps — may be perplexing. Be conscious that these are concrete body images that may add to the child's fears, and try to communicate with the child in specific and concrete ways. If you tell your child your heart is breaking, he may worry about your health. A remark such as "I can't stand it around this house anymore" may mean to the child that she's at fault, that her actions are intolerable.

Even the words *marriage* and *divorce*, which are abstract concepts, are given concrete definitions by the preschool child.

Rita Turow, a writer on the subject of divorce, reports the following conversation between two four-year-olds:

PATTY: A divorce is when somebody goes away from your house.
ELISE: My brother goes away. He goes to school.
PATTY: No, it's not like that. It's for daddies. They go away and never never come back except once in a while. Tommy's mother went away. She's a divorce too. Now I'm a divorce.
ELISE: I want my turn. I want to be a divorce.

Another abstract word, *family,* is usually defined by the preschool child as all the living beings in the house, including pets. The concrete *house,* rather than the relationship, seems to be the most important criterion in the definition of *family,* so it's not easy for the child to understand that a nonresident parent can still be part of the family. The word *father* in the child's mind refers to a specific person in his daily life, a man who lives in his house. That this same person, still to be called *father,* will not live in the child's house requires a shift in his ideas. To the preschool child the family has a specific composition: there is a mother, a father, and a child, or children, as the case may be. Now suddenly this composition is to be altered. The child associates certain functions with each parent and therefore wonders about the reassignment of family tasks. He is apt to worry about who will do what for him, particularly those tasks that have been done by the now absent parent: "Who will make my lunch?" "Who will pick me up at Cub Scouts?" "Who will take me to the barber?" He needs to know he'll be taken care of.

Since the preschooler's concept of her family and family relationships is egocentric, she cannot envision a parent having a familial relationship with another person outside the present structure. One four-year-old asked, "Why doesn't

Daddy live with us?" "Because he has a new wife" was the reply. "Why can't he live here with his new wife?" The child's mother, although taken aback by the suggestion, repeated, in very concrete terms, "Because Daddy and I are divorced. We don't live in the same house anymore."

Time, another abstract concept, is also conceived by pre-schoolers in concrete terms. They know there's nap time, snack time, television time, and bedtime. Their time is now, and talk about the future — next year, next week, summer vacation — has little meaning to them. They cannot grasp the concept of a permanent arrangement. Talking to pre-schoolers about parental visits that will take place every week, every holiday, doesn't mean much in these children's scheme of things.

Another difficult idea to grasp is the finality of the decision that one parent will move. Preschoolers will be better able to understand plans if you make them definite and concrete. As soon as possible take them to visit the place where the departing parent will live. Instead of saying, "Don't worry, Dad will visit with you often," you might say, "Dad will pick you up after the cartoons on Saturday" or "When Mom comes to get you Friday after school, she'll ring the bell three times."

Also be aware of some emotional reactions common during this period. From the very beginnings of life, attachment to a specific person, sometimes a mother, sometimes another person, seems vital to security and comfort. As children grow, they learn to tolerate separation from this person as long as they feel the person is accessible: just watch the two-year-olds in a playground periodically checking in with their mothers. With age children tolerate longer and longer separations, but the whereabouts of parents are still of great concern to the preschooler.

Preschoolers develop strong attachment and affectional ties to the parent of the opposite sex. Freud suggested that some children daydream about how the rival parent will magically

vanish, leaving the desired parent for them. If in fact separation does occur during this stage, the child sees his fantasy
come true: he has his parent all to himself. He may then believe that he has caused the rift and so get a distorted and
inflated picture of his own power. Indeed, some children,
carrying this idea one step further, feel that since they had
the power to cause the break, they also have the power to
bring the parents back together again. Eight-year-old Carrie
recalls: "When I was younger I said, 'Where's Daddy?' And
she [my mother] said, 'He doesn't live with us anymore,' and I
said, 'Oh, well, why don't you marry him?,' and I said that
to my father, too. I just kept trying and I kept getting the
same reply. And now I'm older. I don't try to put them back
together again because I can't. It's like trying to clean up
spilt milk with a spoon."

Between the ages of two and four, a time when some
children develop imaginary friends, a child may talk to her
absent parent as though she were still there. She may even
become annoyed if somebody sits in her parent's chair; she
may insist on including her absent parent in family conversations or expeditions. This is not an uncommon occurrence
and usually disappears with time.

As young children try to make the absent parent into a
concrete image, they are able to think only in extremes. They
may envision one parent as an idol and the other as a monster. This is easy to do, since what often happens is that the
visiting parent appears to be more generous: this parent arrives laden with gifts, while the resident parent, more involved with mundane routine, administers the discipline. In
a two-parent home, through ongoing, daily contact, children
are able to check out and amend their ideas about their parents; with time and a variety of experiences, they discover
that parents are neither idol nor monster all the time. It's
therefore extremely important for children of divorced parents to continue, as much as possible, in close contact with

each parent in many contexts and situations. This will help them experience a wide range of emotions in relation to each parent, not only the extreme ones of love and hate. In the Children of Divorce Project, the preschoolers were the ones who had the strongest reactions to divorce. The finding is not unexpected, since at this age both understanding and ways of coping with problems are limited. Reactions included heightened anxiety at the time of any separation, excessive clinging to the remaining parent, turning to earlier sources of comfort, such as a soft toy, seeking more physical contact, having temper tantrums, and regressing in toilet training. Regression was also shown in the types of questions the young children asked. They reverted to questions, typical of a younger age, aimed at identifying and naming things (What's this? What goes over here?) as they struggled to reassure themselves that their surroundings would remain the same.

For preschool children, divorce means a change in daily routines; they cannot understand the real causes of the separation or the arrangements for custody and visitation. Underlying their questions are the fears that one or both parents no longer love them, that they will be alone, that no one will take care of them, and that they in fact might be responsible for the trouble. Your answers should stress the concrete rather than the abstract, the immediate rather than the past, the practical effect rather than the cause.

Common preschool questions

Don't quote our suggested answers verbatim, since they merely serve as examples. Find the responses best suited to your own feelings and style and family needs, and express them in your own words; discard suggestions you're not comfortable with. Don't tell your children more than they want to know: wait for further questions and take your lead from them. The child will probably ask the same questions again and again in one form or another, so don't give all the information in one fell swoop. This is only the beginning of a dialogue that will extend over a period of time. We've suggested the words; you write the music by putting in your own feelings.

What's a divorce?
"A divorce means we aren't going to live together in the same house anymore."
Why are you getting a divorce?
"We're not happy with each other."
"You've seen us fight and have arguments. Sometimes we get angry with each other. Remember, we're not angry with you. We think it will be better for all of us, and we'll all be happier if Dad and I live in separate houses."
Are you going to divorce me?
"You're not getting a divorce. Mom and I are getting a divorce. We're not happy with each other, but we're happy with you. You're one of the good parts of our lives."
What will happen to me?
"You're our child. You always will be. Daddy will always be your daddy. Mommy will always be your mommy. You'll always have us to take care of you."
Will Mommy go, too?
"Mom is staying here in this house with you. She's not going away. You're going to live in your room in this house. In Dad's house there will be a special place for you." (Be specific about the arrangement that will be made.)
Will Daddy come home for supper?
"No, Daddy will not come here for supper. But lots of times you'll have supper with Daddy at his house or in a restaurant."
Who will fix my bike (braid my hair, make my lunch, and so on)?

"Dad will do lots of things for you. He'll be able to fix your bike [or whatever specific function the child is referring to]. He'll see you often and you'll talk to each other on the telephone. And don't forget, there are many things you do for yourself. But whenever you need help, either Dad or I will help you." (If the departing parent will not be available, assure the child you will be there to help.)

If Daddy loves me, why is he going away?

"He's going away because he and I aren't happy with each other and we want to live apart. You'll live here, but both of us will still take care of you. That's what loving you means. It means taking care of you and being with you."

If I'm good will he stay? Is he going because I was bad?

"He's not going because you were bad. It's not your fault that we're getting a divorce. Sometimes you're bad. All children are bad sometimes. But that's not why Daddy's going. He's going because Daddy and I aren't getting along with each other, and we've decided to live in separate houses. I know you feel mixed up about it, but whenever you're wondering about it, you ask me, and we'll talk about it."

Will Daddy get a new boy?

"You'll always be Daddy's boy, and he'll always be your daddy."

What will happen if I'm sick?

"We'll take care of you just as we always do. When you get sick we'll call the doctor and take care of you and give you medicine and help you get well."

Are we getting divorced from Grandma and Grandpa, too?

"No, they'll always be your grandma and grandpa."

Middle Childhood

The school-age child, from about six to twelve, has wider contacts, acquires more information about people, and his relationships with his peers assume more importance in his life than before he went to school. After a divorce he may worry about whether he can still invite friends to his house or what his friends will think of him and his family. He has opportunities to compare his family situation with that of his friends. Owing to the modern frequency of parental separation and divorce, it's likely that he will know children whose parents have been divorced, so his situation will not necessarily be unique; in fact, in some large-city neighborhoods, to have two parents living together is the unusual case. Nevertheless, there are still places where divorce is not common, and children can be sensitive to the fact that their family composition is not the conventional one.

These are the feelings of two nine-year-olds, as expressed in a group discussion. The participants were boys who had no contact with their fathers.

"The kids don't know my father isn't around. I tell them I do have a father, but he's away on a trip."

"I tell kids my father died in the war when I was young and I never even saw him."

Recent research has shown that although elementary-school-age children are better able than preschoolers to cope with feelings and fears, their concerns show up in other ways. Younger children are apt to show regressive and dependent behavior, whereas children of six to ten are more likely to change their school behavior.

Terry, eight: "It's changed my life a little bit. Without my father, I can't learn that much. So it changed me a lot in school."

Some children become anxious and cannot mobilize the energy and concentration necessary for learning. Despite the greater maturity of the school-age child, concerns typical of the younger child may be reactivated in times of stress. They may fear abandonment and need to be reassured that both parents love them and will continue to take care of them, that they, the children, are not responsible for the break, and that the children, unfortunately, cannot effect a reconciliation.

At a deeper level, a father's or mother's leaving may mean to the child that he's not a lovable person: if his parents no longer love each other, they may stop loving him. Kelly and Wallerstein quote an eleven-year-old: "They keep saying that things will be better, but it's not true. The divorce may be better for them, but not for me. Why can't I live with both of them when I want to so much? Why can't they love each other when it's so important to me? Why can't I do anything about it?"

Even the school-age child will fantasize that her parents may reunite.

Carrie, ten: "Probably the only way I could try and get them back together is to get them in some place, wait until they started fighting, and throw myself into the argument, and try to get one person to see the other person's point of view."

Sally, eight: "I would tell my father that I was really sick or something and then he would come. That would be a way to get him out here. Then I would ask him to talk about it and try to think of a way to get them back together."

Tony, nine: "I would be happy if my parents would get back together. I would wake up in the morning and get into my father's bed and he would kiss me. Then he would go to work and say, 'See you later, alligator,' and I would say, 'In a while, crocodile.' I miss him. I wish I had equal time."

It's crucial to encourage children of this age to show anger, even to express feelings of shame. But don't force them if they're reluctant. Their time will come.

Since they now know about time, money, and societal and other influences, give school-age children specifics about the separation plans, living arrangement, visiting, and financial matters. However, don't overexplain. Many parents, reacting to their own feelings of guilt, tend to burden children with personal details or make disparaging remarks about each other.

Assuring children that they are not the cause of their parents' separation has a reverse side: it's also important not to let them think that the separation is the cause of some of their own behavior. Try and avoid attitudes and remarks such as "Of course, you don't want to join Little League. After all, you don't have a father" or "No wonder your homework isn't done. You don't have a mother to help you."

It is the rare divorce in which the children don't hear angry conversations. Anger is there and they'll know it. But when parents use a child as a weapon or pawn in their ongoing war, the child may feel enraged at both parents.

There are times when the parting parent really does show little interest in the child. Can the remaining parent continue to talk in positive terms about such neglect? If the behavior of one parent is in dramatic contradiction to the description by the other parent, the child may distrust both parents. To continue to make excuses for the parent who doesn't phone, doesn't show up, doesn't remember birthdays and school events — not to mention support checks — communicates to the child that the truth is being kept from him. On the other hand, gratuitous and damaging remarks such as "Your father was always a cheapskate," or "Your mother never gave a damn about anybody but herself," or "You must have learned that from your mother" may be puzzling to the child and lead her to wonder why her parents got married in the first place. Thus, a realistic acknowledgment of the situation, although undoubtedly painful to the child, will help the child face the facts rather than keeping alive a hope for something not likely to occur.

Typical questions in middle childhood

How can she leave if she loves me?

"Mom's leaving is not connected with loving you. She's

leaving because we've had many disagreements and arguments. You've heard some of them. Lots of times we've probably been angry with you because we've been upset with each
other. It's not your fault."

"Mom's leaving because the two of us are unhappy and
can't get along with each other anymore. We love you as
much as ever and we always will."

"Mom loves you the same as she always did. The trouble
is between Mom and me, not between you and either one of
us."

Why is she doing this to me? Did I do something to her?

"I know you probably feel that sometimes you do things
that make us angry, and you might think that's what we've
been fighting about. But that's not the way it is. We're not
separating because of anything that you've done. In fact, most
of the time we're very proud of you and the things you do.
You're the reason for a lot of our good feelings."

"You haven't done anything to make us separate. There
are some things that happen in life that just happen no matter what you do. This is one of them."

"We're not doing this to you personally. We've thought it
over very carefully. It's not an easy decision, but we think it
will be best for all of us, for the whole family."

"We've stayed together for a long time, because we love
you. But now we think we'll be better off if we separate."

*Why are you getting a divorce? Why can't we all stay to-
gether?*

"We haven't been a happy family lately. I think you've felt
that, too. We need to make a change, and we feel this will
make things better for all of us."

"I know you feel worried about the changes we're making,
but you might even like some things about this divorce.
There won't be fighting. You'll have two places to visit, think
of that."

"I know this is hard to understand, and it takes a lot of

getting used to. That's why we'll have to think about it and talk about it a lot."

Why didn't you do something to make her stay? It's your fault!

"There's nothing I can do to stop what's happening. It's not the fault of just one of us. The trouble has been caused by both of us."

"Grownups can make mistakes, too. We're not perfect. Nobody is. Now we know that we made some mistakes. We think that living apart is the best way to correct our mistakes."

"I want him to stay, but he won't."

What did you fight about?

Your answer will depend on the circumstances, but tell the truth if possible.

"It was about drink [or money, or jobs]." If alcoholism or gambling or drug addiction is the reason for the divorce, the children should be told many of the effects of these problems, some of which they have undoubtedly witnessed. Try to convey that this behavior is not deliberate on the part of the parent but rather an illness. Stress the efforts already being made to help, such as participation in therapy groups, counseling, or other appropriate action.

"We don't really love each other anymore, and Mom has been seeing another man."

"We didn't agree about a lot of things. That's what's making us both unhappy. When we get angry and upset with each other, there are times when we don't act nicely to you. But remember, even if we're angry, we still love you. We all have angry feelings sometimes, even with people we love, but we can't *act* loving all the time. Every family has disagreements, but now we feel we can't work things out."

In some instances it may not be appropriate to provide children with the reasons for the divorce, since the parents may not want relatives and neighbors to find out the details.

They can be told that there's going to be a divorce and given fuller information in the future.

What's the use of getting married if you're going to get divorced anyway? Why did you get married in the first place? "We once loved each other but now we disagree more than we agree. Nowadays we're angry and fighting most of the time. Whenever we make up, it doesn't last, and all our disagreements get started all over again."

Will you stop talking to each other? "No. We'll always be members of the family even though we're not living in the same house. Don't forget, we'll always be making plans together for you. But that doesn't mean we'll live together again. We've decided to separate for good, and we won't change our minds."

What if something happens to Mom? "Listen, Mom and I expect to live for a long time, even after you're grown up. But if something unexpected should happen to me or to Mom, there will always be somebody to take care of you."

"It's not very likely that anything will happen to Dad. But you also have Grandma, Aunt Sadie, and Cousin Jarvis, who all love you. Even children who have no relatives or friends at all to take care of them can live in a special home or school. No child is left with absolutely nobody to take care of him or her."

"Remember, you won't always be a child, who needs somebody to look after him. You're going to be able to take care of yourself and maybe even have your own children, and then you'll take care of them."

Brett's parents get along. Why can't you be like them? "For one thing, we really don't know how happy or unhappy Brett's parents are. It's hard to know about other families. We don't know what their real feelings are. You know lots of children whose parents are living together, but you

also know lots of children whose parents don't live together."
"Families can live in different ways. Some do better living
apart and some do better living together. I'm going to be
happier when Dad and I live separately. If I'm happier, I
know I can be a better parent."

Will she ever come back?
"You know you're going to see Mom lots of times. You're
going to see her every weekend and every vacation [or whatever the case may be]. You'll talk to each other as much as
you want to. Mom will come here to visit with you, but she
won't be coming back to live."

*What about money? How will we manage? What about my
allowance?*
The answer to this question will obviously vary according
to your individual circumstances. Tell the children about the
general financial situation in the family. Tell them if there
is going to be no change, if you're changing jobs, if you're
going to work outside the home, if it will be necessary to
move. Assure them that no matter what, arrangements will
always be made for their care.

Did you ever love each other?
"We loved each other very much when we decided to get
married. We wanted to live together and do lots of things
together. We were very happy and we wanted children. Part
of loving each other was having you. There are still good
things in our lives, and you're at the top of that list. But over
the years we've grown in different ways, and things have
changed. They didn't work out the way we wanted. We feel
we don't love each other anymore. That doesn't mean that we
don't love you. We still do and we always will. We've tried
to work things out to stay together, but there doesn't seem to
be any way we can do that. We feel it's better for all of us if
we separate at this time in our lives."

What can I tell my friends?
"If you like, you can say pretty much what we've been

saying to you, that Mom and I aren't happy together and we're going to live apart. Think about it, and if you're not comfortable saying that, you can always say you'd really rather not talk about it. That's your privilege."

What will we do on Thanksgiving?

Many children become concerned about holidays, particularly those that emphasize family ties — Thanksgiving, Christmas, Chanukah, Easter, Passover. Let the children know that the holidays will be celebrated. Some families arrange for two celebrations, some celebrate with each parent on alternate years, some parents join for the holidays, others work out arrangements with grandparents or other relatives.

Adolescence

The adolescent, involved with peers and interests outside the home, is less likely to see the divorce as directed against him personally, and its effect is less devastating than it can be for the younger child. Since adolescents are capable of observing the contradictions and absurdities in the behavior of human beings, they are also capable of understanding how even a parent may be fallible and act unwisely. They are also able to envision alternative styles of family life.

Yet, even though adolescents have developed more internal and social resources, they usually have adverse reactions to divorce. If they have been exposed to repeated scenes and recriminations between parents, they may come to think disparagingly of members of the opposite sex. To protect themselves against pain, they may avoid intimate relationships with peers altogether. An important adolescent struggle is the establishment of independence, but often the remaining parent, governed by the need to depend on somebody, will openly or subtly discourage the teen-aged son or daughter from reaching out for independence, thus compounding the adolescent's conflict. And even the teen-ager needs to be reassured that it is with each other that his parents are unhappy, not with him. The sixteen-year-old who worries about who will pay her college tuition is showing the same anxiety as the four-year-old who wonders who will fix her bike.

*   *   *

The choices for divorcing parents are not ideal. The child will be hurt if the parents remain in an unhappy marriage, and the child will be hurt by the divorce process. Most children, however, after an initial period of readjustment, regain their regular developmental pace. Among those who do not are some who were already having difficulties; divorce is only one of many factors that influence a child's life. Growing up is not easy, divorce or no. As Louise Despert says in her book *Children of Divorce,* "A child who has been able, with his parent's or outside help, to weather a divorce has a better chance for healthy maturity than a child of unhappy marriage who has not come through the stormy experience . . . divorce need not be a bad thing or a good thing. It is only what the human beings involved may make of it . . ."

4

New Relationships and Remarriage

> *Her mother died when she was young,*
> *Which gave her cause to make great moan;*
> *Her father married the worst woman*
> *That ever lived in Christendom.*
>
> — THE BALLAD OF KEMP OWYNE

SHADES OF Cinderella, Snow White, and Hansel and Gretel! The wicked-stepmother myth lives on. Brenda Maddox, author of *The Half-Parent,* writes of her own experience: "I was driving the two girls home from a birthday party and was deep in my fantasy of myself as suburban matron, chauffeuring a carload of kids, while they were silent in the back. Suddenly the friend asked, in a crystal British voice, 'Is that your *stepmother?*' The answer came, slightly shaky, 'yes.' There was a pause. 'Oh. I always thought a stepmother was something like a witch.'"

New mates bear on their shoulders the weight of all the folklore and tales from around the world that cast stepparents in the role of wicked, rejecting, cruel rivals. Since 75 percent of divorced Americans remarry or form new relationships, obviously a large number of children have to accommodate to a parent's new partner.

Some professionals believe the terms *stepmother* and *stepfather* have come to be so onerous that they use phrases such as *new mommy* and *new daddy*. Jessie Bernard, the sociologist, refers to *acquired parents* and *acquired children*. But despite these attempts at escaping the implications of the myth, *step-* remains the prefix most commonly used.

In one-third of American remarriages both partners have children, and so they know firsthand what family life is like and the intensity of the feelings that may be triggered by the introduction of a new person. Even experienced adults in their midforties who consider themselves mature can be intimidated by the thought of stirring up adverse reactions. The father of two children told of his decision to marry a woman with three children: "We knew we were going to be married soon after we met. We were dynamite together. We made the decision, and then suddenly we became petrified of the children."

These are the reactions of children to the idea of stepparents:

Linda, twelve: "At first I didn't mind when my father saw his girl friend, as long as it wasn't all the time. It shook me up sometimes, because my mother used to be in her place. I feel a little bit jealous of them, and I still hope that I have that Friday afternoon with him alone."

Fred, nine: "I wouldn't mind if he got married, except if that person had kids, because my father might spend more time with them."

Tim, ten: "My father is remarried but I don't want to meet his wife. She might be an idiot and she might not be. I don't know."

Tonia, ten: "If my mother ever got remarried, I don't think I'd call the guy Dad. I don't know if I could feel right calling him by his first name, either. I'd probably just call him 'hey you!'"

John, nine: "I wouldn't feel bad if my mother got married again, but I wouldn't feel good, either."

Josh, nine: "I'm going to try to help her find somebody if she wants to marry, because she says, 'All right, Josh, you'll be the first person I tell.' She says I'm the man of the house. That makes me feel good. It makes me feel important."

Adults, when asked to recall memories of their parents' remarriage, usually remember two events vividly: first, the time they were told their parents were splitting up, and second, when they found out that one parent was going to remarry. Some resented not being told until after the remarriage took place. One woman said, "I heard them talking to my aunt and going over their marriage plans. My mother never said anything at all to me about it, and I wondered why. I got the feeling that she didn't consider my feelings worth considering."

This leads to the first of our general guidelines for handling the subject of a new relationship.

General Guidelines

1. Let the children know your plans and let them get to know the new person in their lives. Try and arrange for your children and the new person to spend some time together, both with and without you. Don't go overboard. Wooing the child holds out the promise of a privileged relationship that's not likely to occur in actuality. Special treatment may give the child the impression that she has more power in the relationship than is true.

2. Don't ask the children's permission. At first this may sound like a good way to involve them and to make sure they accept the new parent. Wrote one movie star in her autobiography, "I said, children, go to bed and discuss it between yourselves and before you go back to camp, you tell me what you think, and it was a unanimous decision. So I telephoned

my fiancé, and I said, 'Well, if you're still in favor of the idea, I'll marry you.' "

Attractive as this may seem, most therapists don't feel it's a good idea. They believe the decision to marry is a parental responsibility; involving the children in the decision-making process places too great a burden on them.

3. Aim for equal treatment. The stereotype that the stepparent's own children are treated better than the stepchildren may become a fact. This is a letter received by a newspaper that runs a "What's Your Problem?" column written by and for elementary-school children: "As we're getting older, my stepfather hates us more and more. All he cares about is his own two kids. My brother and me always get yelled at. He sits around all day and gives orders, but he lets his kids get away with murder. We're afraid to say anything to my mother because we don't know if she'll get mad. We're thinking about leaving home. Do you have any advice at all?"

Sometimes the situation works in reverse, as discussed in the following guideline.

4. Avoid the "guilty stepparent" trap. The self-conscious stepparent, sensitive to possible accusations of favoritism, rejection, usurpation of a loved parent, is all too ready to plead guilty. Fearing that an audience is watching to see if they will in fact be cruel, such stepparents bend over backwards to be kind to their spouse's children, and the "superparent" backlash sets in.

"I never hit my stepchildren but I clobber my own."

"Every time I yell at my stepchildren I feel guilty and try to make it up to them. I don't obsess about it when I yell at my own children. I just let it happen and then it blows over."

Remember that in any family, reconstituted or otherwise, feelings of love, hate, jealousy, frustration, and aggression exist. It's not perfect in your nondivorced neighbor's house, either. Be as fair as seems reasonable to you.

5. Admit your feelings. Natural parents don't always love

their children wholeheartedly; in fact, it's an unrealistic expectation. If stepparents could also be encouraged to accept their ambivalent feelings, a lot of tension might be avoided. Some parents comment:

"I've never gone in for this hogwash that there's no difference between my wife's children and our own together. Of course there's a difference . . ."

"I didn't want to make demands on them, but then I harbored a lot of resentment afterwards."

"I wanted them to like me so I bought them things and then I was sore because I didn't have money left over."

6. Define your role. Set some ground rules with your new mate. Knowing that you share basic beliefs about child rearing will help during the inevitable times of conflict. Children whose lives have been touched by death or divorce usually spring back, but there's first a transition time, when extra patience and mutual support come in handy. Be clear on your roles and what you expect of each other. Here's how four stepparents defined their roles:

"I try to act like an older sister."

"It's a compromise relationship at best."

"We're something like cousins, related, but not too close."

"I'm a quasi-parent."

You're not the child's real parent. You can't re-create the old family. But you can offer the child warmth, hospitality, friendship, and a special relationship. Says Brenda Maddox, "Stepfamilies can be happy, even happier than families in which there has never been more than one mother or father, but it takes more work. A stepparent cannot be the same as a real parent . . . Yet there are compensations for the strains. My own particular reward has been to help two young people who are nothing like me to be more like themselves . . ."

7. Recognize that there's always an absent parent. No marriage that produces a child is ever finally dissolved, whether divorce or death occurs. There's always a parent who lives on

in the child even when not present physically. Some remarrieds comment:

"He [the children's father] never writes. He never visits. But the children look like him, and so I'm constantly reminded of him."

"My wife's first husband lives in London, but the kids have pictures of him around, and the study is full of his books."

Comparisons, invidious or otherwise, are inevitable: "She was some cook," "He was always at the track," "She never came home without stopping at the corner bar," "He could never hold a job." The task of the stepparent is to make peace with the absent parent in a way that will not shake the child's respect. It's not easy, but worth a try and essential for future peace.

8. Go easy on changes. To ease the transition for the children, retain as much of the accustomed routine and surroundings as possible. Many a new parent, in a burst of zeal, tries to upgrade the children's lives, even if only in rearranging their room. Although the motives may be the highest, the risk is that the children may view this as an interference or even disapproval of a former way of life.

Some Developmental Considerations

Experts agree that children under three and near-adult children are the ones who are most accepting of a new parent.

Children under three have many unverbalized questions, which you can respond to most effectively in nonverbal ways — by providing physical contact, familiar surroundings and possessions, the security of a predictable routine.

With children over three new relationships stir up some old concerns and create some brand-new ones. Common worries include: Will she take my father away from me?, Will I be able to see my real mother?, Will he love her more than me?, Will they have a baby? A remarriage dashes a child's hope for a parental reconciliation, and for some children a conflict of loyalties ensues: they may feel they're betraying the remaining parent if they like the new partner of the remarrying parent. In addition, they have to make room in their emotional lives for another person — not an easy task for anyone.

Psychoanalysts suggest that the stepchild has some special emotional problems to deal with, one of which is the intensification of sexual conflicts. In most children the desire for the parent of the opposite sex and competitiveness with the parent of the same sex are conflicts that occur and are resolved between the ages of three and six and then recur in adolescence. At either of these times, the appearance of a parent's new sexual partner can distress the child. Stepchildren may find the conflict difficult to resolve. Every little girl may want to marry Daddy, but not every little girl actually has to watch when Daddy marries somebody else. Said one six-year-old girl after attending her father's wedding, "I knew all the words, and I wanted to say them but nobody asked me to say anything."

Splitting is a psychoanalytic concept that applies to stepchildren. Splitting refers to a situation in which the feelings of love and hate are "split up" and projected onto two different people: one person is then loved as totally good, and the other person is hated as totally evil. Although this unconscious state is present to some degree in all children, with age most come to adjust to the reality that both their parents are good and rewarding at times and bad and punishing at other times. The stepchild, however, may retain the split and neatly assign all the good qualities to the absent parent and all the bad qualities to the stepparent. Moreover, the child can idealize the parent who is gone and hold the stepparent responsible for all the bad things in the child's life.

"My real mother wouldn't treat me mean like that" or "If

I lived with my father, everything would be O.K." are often-heard refrains. The stepchild has a harder time in coming to understand that it's possible to love and hate the same person. Another task unique to the stepchild is that she has to learn that she can love two parents of the same sex. One stepmother reported that her five-year-old stepson ran to her one day declaring, "Susan, now it's O.K. to love you. Daddy says I can still love Mommy, too."

Still another task for the stepchild is the mourning of an absent or dead parent. Mourning is a complex process, during which the love and hopes that have been associated with the lost person are gradually given up and later redirected to a new person. Mourning in children may take different forms. Some children, in a self-protective way, seem to be detached, or tough, or reserved — all qualities that stepparents may think are directed at them.

Other psychological problems of stepchildren include the need to give up the special closeness often present in a single-parent family. "My mom goes out with this man, and I think she doesn't love me anymore. She never has time for me. What should I do?" writes one forlorn nine-year-old to "Dear Kidsday," an advice column for children in *Newsday*, a Long Island newspaper. Many children have assumed an adult role in the family, and although they may be relieved to give it up, they also may resent losing their special status.

In some cases a new stepparent represents a third, not a second, readjustment. This is true in cases when the child, after the departure of a parent, has been cared for by a house-keeper or a nonparent family member. Thus, when the step-parent arrives and the caretaker leaves, still another separation is necessary. "I'm getting my fourth mother," said one eight-year-old.

Another old concern may be reactivated. Stepchildren know all too well that marriage is a temporary state. Although they may try very hard to get rid of the intruder, they also fear they may succeed. If children feel they were responsible for their parents' divorce, who's to say that it may not happen again? Ten-year-old Arthur: "My mother remarried but she divorced, because my stepfather was always traveling and they never saw each other. All he cared about was bowling. During her wedding I said to myself, 'I hope this one stays with Mom!' And then I found out, 'Nope, he's not going to stay.' When she told me about the divorce I thought to myself, 'Not again!' "

As children struggle to work out new relationships, they can count themselves lucky if they are blessed with a step-parent who is alert to some of their special problems and questions and open to an exchange of ideas. Following are some children's questions typical during the parent's court-ship and remarriage or new living arrangement. Remember, the answers are not intended to be delivered as written. Rather, they are suggestions, and in all cases your next step depends on the response of the child.

Why do you have to go out with ———*?*
"You know you like to go out with your friends and have a good time. I like to do that, too."

"I have a good time with ——— and we like to be to-gether."

"You and I have some good times together, but sometimes we each need to have some time with friends."

The older child can understand: "I've been very lonely and I feel I'd like to be with other people and get to make some new friends."

What do you do together?
"We like to be together. Sometimes we go to the movies, or we meet some friends, or we go to a restaurant."

Is ——— *going to live with us? But how about Dad?*
"Dad and I are not married anymore. ——— and I love

each other and we're going to get married [or live together].
———— is not your father. You'll still see your father every
weekend [or whatever the case may be]."

"Your father and I will always be your parents. ———— is
not going to take your father's place."

Tell the older children more details about the plans for
the marriage or living arrangement. They can understand
that a new family can bring exciting new experiences and
new relationships.

*Why does he have to be part of the family? I've already got a
father.*

"Yes, you're right, you do. ———— isn't going to take his
place and doesn't want to. He just wants to have a good relationship with you and be a special kind of relative to you. He
doesn't ever want to stop you from being with your father.
He's going to be part of the family because he and I love each
other and we want to live together."

Why do you need him when you've got me?

"You and I love each other in a special way and nothing
can change that. There are other kinds of love, too. ————
and I love each other in another way. We love each other
like a husband and wife. That's different from the way a
parent and child love each other. When you grow up you'll
want that kind of love, too."

What should I call him?

"Let's see which name you think fits best." The choice
should depend on the child's preference. It's generally not a
good idea to use the same name the child uses for the biological parent of the same sex. The younger child may prefer
to call the new parent Uncle or Aunt. Older children often
call the new stepparent by his or her first name.

Paul Bohannon, author of *Divorce and After,* believes it is
very important to confirm a stepparent's authority in the
family by having the stepchild address that person in some

parental form. He tells of a nine-year-old girl whose mother had married four times: "She called her father 'Daddy.' The other three she called Daddy-Tom, Daddy-Dick, and Daddy-Harry... Using the first name may undermine a good authority relationship between a stepparent and stepchild and may intensify competition." Make up your mind on this one.

If ——— comes to my graduation, does that mean that Dad won't come?

"No, Uncle Pete doesn't take Dad's place. I'm sure Dad will come if he's able to."

If ——— is going to live here, why don't you get married?

This question is likely to be asked only by an older child.

"Your father and I made some mistakes when we got married. I want to be sure I don't make the same mistakes again. So ——— and I are going to live together so we can get to know each other very well. Then we'll know whether or not we want to get married."

How come Allan teases me all the time because you're not married?

"I'm surprised that Allan thinks that's something to tease about. We know it wouldn't be good for any of us if I made a mistake by marrying. We didn't have an easy time when your father and I split up, and I don't want the same thing to happen again."

And finally, the question most new stepparents are waiting for:

You're not my mother, so why should I do what you say?

"I know I'm not your mother. I'm your father's wife. No one will replace your mother. I don't want to take her place. I can tell you what to do in our house. I'm telling you what I believe is best for you."

For some children, it would be helpful to add some additional reassurance that it's not unusual to feel the way they do: "I know you feel angry, and that's O.K. If you don't like what I say, you can tell me about it and let me know what you think. But, if I still think I'm right you'll have to go along with it." Thus you let the child know that you are functioning as a parent, although not usurping a parent's place. You also let her know that she can be angry with you just as she could be with a natural parent.

The following question was written by a nine-year-old to the "What's Your Problem?" column:

> What should I do? My mother's boyfriend acts like my father. This is what I mean. I came home from school, and I had homework so I sat in the living room and started to do it. But he was watching television. So I started watching television. Was I wrong? He said, "Stop watching television and get your homework done!" Well, I finished my homework and slammed my feet all the way up the stairs. I didn't have time to talk to my mother. Was I wrong?
>
> *Helpless.*

How would you answer "Helpless"?

5

Adoption

"I HAVEN'T decided whether to tell Amy she's adopted. Why should I upset her?"

"John is ours, even more than if I actually gave birth to him. Why does he have to know?"

"Alice is adopted and she knows it. So do all our neighbors and friends. Why should we hide it?"

"If we don't explain it, it will always be in the background and can be very harmful. But why can't we wait till she's older?"

Questions about adoption seem to raise the parental anxiety level more than any other sensitive topic. In this case many parents do some reverse thinking. While they may encourage their children's questions in general, regarding questions as a sign of intelligence, when it comes to questions about adoption they start to worry about their competence as parents. In fact, some parents start worrying about how to answer questions during the child's infancy. In a program conducted by the Children's Home in Cincinnati, adoptive parents were asked to list the topics most worrisome to them. Heading the list were: How and when to tell a child about the adoption and how to interpret the facts about the biological parents.

It is hardly surprising that most adoptive parents are highly self-conscious about the whole procedure. In order to adopt their child, they have had to be analyzed, interviewed, processed, and computerized. They've had to face a lot of hard issues even before the adoption took place. They've been influenced by the attitudes of their community, which range from negative and critical to supportive. They've been flooded with material generated by the media about the joys, sorrows, and hazards of adoption. They've had to sort out their own feelings about such weighty, emotionally charged issues as fertility, unwed parenthood, religious and ethnic heritage, and undesirable character traits genetically transmitted to children.

Many adults who themselves were adopted as children remember vividly how their questions about adoption were handled. They agree that it is crucial to tell children the truth and that the adoptive parents should be the ones to tell it. Those who found out about their adoption from another family member, a friend, pediatrician, or neighbor usually experienced much pain. What they had wanted in childhood was a clearer picture of the facts: information that would help them picture their birth parents in a favorable light, without the implication that they were unwanted or rejected children. These adults reflect on how they found out about their adoption:

"When I was ten my aunt told me I had been adopted. My parents became very upset and denied it. Some days I felt I belonged to the family and some days I didn't."

"I was told, starting when I was about three, that I was something called adopted because of the following chain of events: When I was born, both my parents died (both parents dying in childbirth?) and a lady took care of me. Meanwhile, my mother and father wanted a baby and found the one baby who was just right for them, and that was you-know-who . . . I was perfectly aware I was breaking a tacit family rule by beginning to ask certain questions — How old were my parents when they died? What did they die of? Why didn't anyone else in their families take me in?"

Until recently, parents were advised to speak about adoption as early as possible, as soon as the child could respond to language and to the emotional tone that accompanies it. The reason for this advice was that the child's earliest associations with the word *adopted* would evoke warm and positive feeling. However, subsequent investigations have shown that early telling often results in an artificial emphasis on adoption, which sets the child apart from others. Moreover, children's inability to understand fully can cause distortions and misconceptions and arouse fears that they are unable to handle at an early age.

Another reason parents were advised to tell children about adoption when the children are very young was that they might hear the news first from an outsider. Current opinion is that even if this does happen at an early age it need not be earthshaking. To young children the word *adoption* itself has little meaning; they may forget it, or may ask about it. Parents can then speak about adoption in a matter-of-fact way, in the simple language appropriate to the child's age. A catastrophic response is likely to occur only if parents overreact. If your three- or four-year-old says, "Pete says I'm adopted," you should calmly reply, "You are." If your child then says, "What's 'adopted'?," you can say, "That's one of the ways a child comes into a family," and wait for further questions.

Many experts in the field of adoption believe that giving too much information early in the child's life may relieve the parent's anxiety, but it may place a burden on the child. Telling five-year-olds that their biological parents could not take care of them is difficult to deal with for several reasons — children at this age cannot understand and differentiate the motivations of other people, and they may think that if one set of parents couldn't take care of them, perhaps it will happen again with the present set of parents.

So-called expert advice has been confusing. It is unlikely

that anyone can prescribe the exact way for all parents to deal
with questions of adoption. It is our plan to provide some
developmental data to help you respond to questions in ways
that are comfortable for you and at the same time are com-
patible with the needs of your child at particular ages. Remember, children's needs and capacity for understanding do
not remain fixed; information they can understand at one
time may be meaningless to them or even detrimental at another time. Few questions on any important topic remain
answered once and for all, and adoption questions are no
exception. Questions will arise at different times, in different
words, and in different contexts, asked of different people. No
doubt the news that one is adopted has major impact and sets
off a process of reflection, inquiry, and readjustment on the
part of the child. However, when the child's feelings are respected, when questions are answered with honesty and empathy, the experience need not be traumatic. On the contrary,
it can offer the growing child unique opportunities for self-
examination and the development of a positive sense of self.

What questions are likely to arise at different ages? Let's
consider cognitive and emotional growth in three periods —
the preschool age, middle childhood, and adolescence — emphasizing those concepts relevant to adoption.

The Child Under Five

The world of the child of this age is permeated by egocen-
trism. This refers to the child's inability to place herself in
the position of another person, to play the role of another
person, or to see the world from the perspective of another
person. (You might be interested in referring to this concept
and its effect on the young child's thinking as we discussed it
in the chapter on divorce.)

In the magical world of the young child, anything is possible. One three-year-old we interviewed had a cousin named Ginger who went away to summer camp. When her neighbor two weeks later bought a dog, which he named Ginger, the girl believed that her cousin Ginger had turned into the dog Ginger. Children at this age may believe themselves capable of performing such feats as being in two places at the same time and of communicating with inanimate things. Many parents are familiar with the imaginary friends conjured up by their children and endowed with a specific reality and a specific set of characteristics.

Understanding relationships

We sometimes forget that words carry different meanings for child and adult. Don't assume that you and your child always share a common vocabulary. Often a word has a personal and literal meaning for the child. For example, the word *uncle,* for most adults, refers to a family relationship. Yet many young children think it's merely part of the name of a person — Uncle Charlie — rather than a description of a relationship. When we asked six-year-old Cathy what an uncle was, she hesitated and then said, "He's sort of like an extra person around in case your grandma dies." The relationships expressed by words such as *uncle* are abstract concepts. Similarly, adoption is an abstract concept and presupposes understanding that is beyond the thinking capacity of a five-year-old.

Affecting their ability to understand family relationships is young children's difficulty in dealing with more than one concept at a time. In order for a child to understand her relationship to her mother she must be able to coordinate two ideas. First, she must know that her mother is a member of a group of women called mothers; at the same time the child must consider a second idea, her particular relationship to her mother, that of a child.

The young child also has trouble in perceiving people in

more than one role. This is illustrated by an experiment in which children were asked the following question: "The mother studied and became a doctor. Is she still a mother?" Fifty-eight percent of the five- to seven-year-olds answered that she is not. They couldn't conceive of one person performing two functions.

The child who learns the word *mother* knows that the word refers to her own mother and then generalizes and applies the word to all women: *mother* and *woman* are the same. Similarly, friendly toddlers endow most men with the title *Daddy*.

It seems unreasonable to expect a young adopted child to understand that she came from a person called a mother but not the particular person she calls Mother. Equally hard for her to understand is the idea that there might be a woman who cannot be a mother. For the child to comprehend that an unknown, unseen woman is her biological mother or that she was once inside another woman's body is simply too complex a set of ideas to handle at an early age. Said four-year-old Brett when he was told he grew inside a woman's body, "Why would I do that?"

Although children use the word *family,* they are not sure of its exact meaning. Precisely what makes a person a relative is hazy in the mind of the preschooler. A four-year-old may define a grandmother as a person "who comes to the house and gives you things." Although children use words such as *family, uncle, grandma,* they do not grasp their exact meaning in relation to family members.

Understanding the past

Young children cannot relate to the events, either emotional or physical, that preceded or surrounded their birth. The word *birthday* becomes part of every child's vocabulary at an early age, and we assume that a child knows what a birthday commemorates, that we're all talking about the same thing.

Not so. If we ask young children to define *birthday*, we get some surprising answers: "It's when everybody comes to your house," "It means you have a party," "It means you're now five." From the child's point of view, a birthday means a specific event and does not symbolize anything. Young children believe that the day on which a birthday falls can be any day and is chosen at random by their parents. It can occur any number of times, not related to the passage of a year.

Adults often show children photographs of family members extending over a period of years. However, young children do not understand that people change and look different as time passes. They cannot comprehend that the person in the picture who looks so different is the same person they know as Mother or Father. The past has little meaning for them. Only when children begin to perceive that events have causes and that relationships are complex, and to grasp the nature of the passage of time, can they think about their past. A concern with origins, a time before one existed, requires a level of cognitive maturity that does not occur until about the age of seven.

Sense of identity

The quality of children's care and their social interactions during their first two years of life affect their ability to develop trust in others. Between two and three years of age, children establish a sense of separateness and independence from their caretakers; they discover and assert their individuality. At the same time, they learn to adapt themselves to the expectations and customs of those around them. They learn to use a toilet, go to sleep at a certain time, say hello and good-by, even though at times they may not want to do any of these things.

According to Freud, children between the ages of three and six enter the "oedipal phase," in which children see themselves as the partner of the parent of the opposite sex and the rival of the parent of the same sex. Children become involved in a conflict; they experience both affection and resentment toward their parents, and often strong feelings of love, anger, and fear are aroused. In Freud's theory, the oedipal conflict is resolved through identification with the parent of the same sex. (See page 28.)

As children identify and model themselves on their parents, they come to share many things with them. They may be told they look like their father or mother, they adopt their parents' attitudes and points of view. Experts in child development feel that overemphasis on adoption during this period may interfere with the identification with the parents. Identification may occur when it is stressed to children that they grew inside another woman or that their father is another man, not the parent they live with. To children at this stage of emotional development, the message that their biological parents relinquished them, no matter how carefully phrased and explained, often means that somehow it was the children's fault — they were unwanted because they were bad or ugly or nasty.

In the view of psychoanalyst Erik Erikson, children face an ever-widening range of human relationships during the course of growing up. According to Erikson, children's significant relationships through the first five years progress from a single mothering figure to both parents to the broader family. Again, parents' emphasizing of the fact that a child has more than one mother may be confusing in the child's process of adapting to a widening sphere of relationships.

Common to all developmental theories is the critical importance of stable family relationships through the early years. During these years, so crucial to the development of identification and a sense of self, premature knowledge that one has two sets of parents may produce distressing conflicts within a child too emotionally or intellectually immature to absorb the facts.

Many children, frustrated and angry with their natural

parents, imagine that they do not really belong in their adoptive family, that these are not their real parents, and that somewhere, waiting in the wings for the right moment to rescue them, are their perfect parents, perhaps a king and a queen. Having two sets of parents enables the adopted child to fantasize that one set of parents is good and one set of parents is bad — the "splitting" referred to in chapter four. Most children have conflicting sets of feelings, but eventually they come to realize that they can live with a wide range of emotional reactions to their parents, that their parents are both loving and frustrating, good and bad. But for the adopted child, reality coincides with fantasy. Her adoptive parents really did get her after she was born, usually of unknown parents. When daily life with the adoptive parents and their shortcomings becomes trying, it's easier to romanticize the image of the natural parents: when the child feels hurt or rejected or angry, she can turn for comfort to the fantasized perfect natural parents. "I can remember as a child when I wouldn't get my way I'd often think I probably would have gotten my way if my real mother had me. I dreamed of her as a fairy godmother, someone who was young and beautiful," said one adult adoptee.

Holding on to these fantasies allows children to avoid dealing with tasks crucial for their development: coming to terms with their mixed negative and positive feelings toward their parents and clearly distinguishing between what is real and what is fantasy. A loving and secure relationship between parents and child helps the child accomplish these tasks.

Middle Childhood — the Elementary-School Years

Had I been told all the little things I wanted to know, or if I had been told that some day the information would be given to me in full, my mind would have been more at rest.

— An adult woman reflecting on her developmental years

Elementary-school-age children want specific details and want to know the reasons behind the explanations they are offered. They clearly know fact from fantasy; they can deal with complex relationships; they perceive cause-and-effect relationships, as in reproduction; their sense of the past is more accurate than when they were preschoolers. Their world is no longer confined to the home and immediate neighborhood; their contacts widen to include schoolmates, teachers, and other people. Friendships assume great importance; as ideas are tried out on peers, attitudes are modified. This is the age at which children can best deal with the facts of their origins and their adoption.

Marjorie, who is twenty-seven, recalls: "There is no greater gift that a nine- or ten-year-old can give a friend than a secret, especially about herself. So, heart palpitating, I one day manipulated my best friend into a state of climactic excitement, and then delivered unto her, 'I am adopted.' 'Oh, that, my mother told me that when we were in the first grade.' It turned out that all my friends knew and were quite bored with the topic." Marjorie gained a new perspective when she discovered that adoption, so secret and so central an issue to her, did not determine the way people related to her.

Some of the same questions posed at an earlier age may reappear, but as children become more sophisticated, the answers can be more complete. Their need for reassurance as to their worth remains constant, however, and should always be considered when responding to questions, not necessarily always in words, but in tone or with an affectionate gesture.

The Adolescent

Adolescents think more abstractly and can imagine what might be, instead of being limited by what is. They can hypothesize, take into account all eventualities, and exhaust all possible solutions to a problem. They have a sense of time passed and can project themselves into the future. In regard to their personal growth, adolescents need to establish themselves outside the family circle as individuals in their own right, a transition usually accompanied by problems and turmoil.

Adopted adolescents may have a particularly stressful time, since their struggle for independence revives old questions about origins and background. Some adolescents search for information about their biological parents, grandparents, and other relatives, especially when few facts have been made known to them. Not all adopted adolescents are burning with curiosity, however; many are satisfied with what they already know and have no interest in finding out more.

Until recently, the adolescent who sought more information was believed to be showing neurotic concerns. Now, however, we respect the desire to know as a basic right, which does not necessarily reflect discontent, a pathological preoccupation with origins, or an unsuccessful relationship with the adoptive parents.

*   *   *

How can this information on the intellectual and emotional development of children help us answer their questions on adoption?

General Guidelines

1. Emotional tone is just as important as the factual information imparted, for it is the tone that conveys your attitudes. Parents all use different words to give information. Feelings of love and respect will always get through even when the words chosen are not always the precise ones children will understand.

2. An open, matter-of-fact attitude helps. The way you handle questions sets the tone for further questions. Negative or evasive responses discourage further probing. An example of a negative response is the one given by an adoptive mother who, when asked by her daughter whether she was adopted, told her to treat the information as a secret: "Don't tell anybody. We want people to think you're ours," she said. Withholding information may encourage the child to fantasize about other unknowns; fantasies may be perpetuated and spread into other areas of the child's life. Silence may mean to the child that something is wrong or sad or bad about being adopted. It is also important for the child to know that many children are adopted, that hers is not a one-of-a-kind situation.

3. Overemphasis can be as detrimental as avoiding or hiding the facts. Constant reminders of the adopted child's status can make the child feel different from others and thus cause anxiety. An adopted person recalls in childhood: "I was told I was adopted from the very beginning, but felt that my parents overdid it by introducing me as 'our specially adopted chosen daughter.' It always embarrassed me, as it drew attention to my being adopted." Being overly conscious of having been "chosen" may also burden the child with the responsibility to be special and perfect at all times.

Overemphasis may also cause the child to get an inflated view of herself and her own power, as well as leave her unprepared for the outside world: "As a child I was treated somewhat like a princess. I was so overprotected and sheltered I had difficulty in adjusting to new situations and new people."

In addition, special treatment can cause considerable resentment on the part of siblings. As one four-year-old natural child said, "Look at me! I'm cute, too!"

4. Keep the answers short and simple for the young child. Try not to tell more than the child wants to know. Over-

explanation obscures the facts. Don't forget, he can always ask more questions, either now or in the future. Let requests for further information come from the child, and be patient with repeated questions. Children often repeat questions for purposes of clarification; repetition is one of the ways they learn.

5. Try to ascertain the real intent of the question. What is the child really asking? As an adult you may attribute to questions meanings that are deeper and more significant than are intended by the child. An example of this is the now proverbial story about the child who asked his mother where he came from and received in detail the story of conception, pregnancy, and birth; he waited patiently and then remarked, "What I mean is, did I come from Chicago or New York?"

When you're not sure what your child is really asking, you might ask her to say it again or to try and say it another way. Asking "What do you think?" is also a way of getting an idea of what she really wants to know. Sometimes she may already know the answer but be looking for reassurance or validation of her perceptions. Knowing what precipitated the question can guide the reply. This is such a dialogue:

FIVE-YEAR-OLD ALEX: Why is Gail's mother fat?
MOTHER: Why do you think she's fat?
ALEX: Because she ate too much.
MOTHER: Is that what you really think?
ALEX: Well, no, I think she's getting a baby.

Since Alex seems to be trying to figure things out, this provides a good opportunity to explain that the baby grows inside the mother. He already knew this but needed to try out the idea and have it confirmed by his mother.

6. Try not to mention adoption when you're upset or angry. Obviously, all parents are at times upset by their children's behavior, but linking anger to the idea of adoption

can undermine the child's feelings of security. Some parents, when frustrated, have reminded the child to be thankful she's adopted. This idea is a difficult one for the child to comprehend, since it deals with events beyond her control. Remarks such as "You're so bad today I wish you were someone else's child!," "Why can't you act like Steven?," "I'm thinking about giving you back," and "If you don't behave we'll send you away" may be experienced as rejection by an adopted child, who has special worries about being abandoned.

7. Keep the lines of communication open. Many adoptees report that they held their curiosity in check and didn't ask questions for fear of hurting their adoptive parents' feelings. They picked up the message that their questions weren't really welcome. In a novel by Jill Robinson, *Perdido,* an adoptive mother says to her child, "Don't punish me with your questions."

Babette Dalshimer, an adoptee who has written extensively on the subject, recalls: "I had been told that nobody, nobody, except my parents, my grandparents, and I knew I was adopted. I do not recall whether I was ever admonished not to tell anyone, but wise child that I was, I knew a dirty secret when I heard one, and I knew that dirty secrets don't get talked about either in the family or out of it."

With a child who seems reluctant to talk or ask questions, try opening the door for her. Be sensitive about your timing. You might say, "Lots of adopted kids wonder about what their birth parents were like. Do you ever wonder?" If the child responds, tell her you'll try to answer as best you can. If she doesn't respond, she's not ready. Don't press; try it at another time.

8. Try to clarify your own feelings on a number of issues related to adoption. You should do this in order to be able to deal with your children's questions in a comfortable way. David Kirk, an authority on adoption and an adoptive par-

ent himself, outlined some difficulties encountered by many adoptive parents. These include:

Feelings of deprivation due to childlessness.

Little contact with other adoptive families, who could serve as models.

No physical pregnancy to serve as emotional preparatory period, and no feedback from friends and relatives regarding parenthood.

Agency screening procedures that put the adoptive parents in the position of being dependent on outside approval.

The situation of being older than most biological parents. (Many adoptive parents have been childless for some time.)

A probationary period following an adoption, which creates uncertainty and fear of losing the child.

No religious or traditional ceremonies that mark the child's arrival.

Circumstances of the child's birth may conflict with the parents' moral values. For example, the child may have been an out-of-wedlock child.

If you're aware of these issues, unique to adoptive families, recognize their importance and discuss them with your spouse, so that you'll be able to communicate with your children.

The ease with which adopted children can question their parents is related to the emotional security of the parents. If you're at home with the issues, you'll be able to convey your attitudes along with the information.

Questions

Here are some specific questions commonly asked by adopted children. The first questions usually occur when the child wonders where babies come from.

Where did I come from? How did I get borned? Whose body did I come from?

A three- to- five-year-old is probably not looking for the story of her adoption, although her parents may think she is, because they've been poised and ready for this question for some time. At this point the most appropriate explanation is that all babies grow in a special place in a woman's body before they are born, usually in a hospital. Questions such as *Did I drink from a bottle? Was I born in a hospital? Did I sleep in a crib? Did I cry? Did I eat baby food? Was I cute? How much did I weigh?* can all be answered with a simple "Yes." As the child begins to build a sense of time passed and to perceive himself growing and changing over time, he wants to know what he was like as a baby.

What's "adopted"?

"That's one way a baby comes into a family."

Often specific questions are likely to arise after the birth of a sibling. One adopted child recalls that he thought his parents were dissatisfied with him and were trying out a new baby. Specific statements that he would always be part of the family reassured him of his continued safe place. Responses should not include all the facts. Tell the story of the adoption gradually and in tune with the child's ability to incorporate the information. There will be numerous opportunities.

After the age of six or seven give information about birth and reproduction in response to the above questions. Describe how life begins for all of us. Facts about adoption can follow facts about birth in general. The full story needs repeating, but it is at about this age that the information seems to be assimilated. The child can now understand her relationship to two women. One explanation might be: "Some babies are taken care of by the people whose egg and seed made them grow, but others aren't. You were born from another woman's body, but I'm your mother, because I take care of you."

Another explanation might be: "We decided we wanted

a child. We knew there are two ways to have a child. One way would be for the baby to grow inside Mother's body, and then the baby would be in our family. The other way is adoption. We could bring home and raise a child in our family who was born from another woman. We wanted to begin [or add to] our family by adoption." This response lets the child know that adoption was a choice, and that she was not the result of default. She can learn about fertility later on.

Vocabulary is important. Use the words *mother* and *father* to mean the adoptive parents. Always use adjectives such as *first, birth, natural,* and *biological* to denote the biological parent. Don't use the terms for the adoptive and the biological parents interchangeably.

Some adopted children think that adoption means they were born in a way different from other children, and it's important to be sure that they know that they, like every child, came from a woman's body. One little girl had been given an explanation similar to those above, that there were two ways to get a baby, one by birth and one by adoption. When she saw her baby brother in the adoption-agency office, she said thoughtfully, "He wasn't born, either."

How did you choose me? How did you get me? What if you chose wrong? Could you give me back?

"The doctor [or agency, or home] took very good care of you. We came and when we saw you we loved you and we took you home. We're all very lucky to be together, and we'll always be a family."

"When parents decide to adopt a baby, they go to a special place called an adoption agency. We went and told them we wanted to adopt a baby. When we heard the baby would be coming soon, we were very excited and happy. We got everything ready. We fixed up the baby's room and we bought clothes and toys. Then we brought you home, and you were happy and so were we."

It's important not to lie. An answer such as "We chose you from all the others because you were the best" is simply not true, and the child will know. Again, if the child thinks he was chosen because of some special qualities, he may feel he has to maintain them, or he'll be rejected. One adolescent recalled that he imagined a supermarket with babies lined up waiting to be chosen by people making the rounds of the aisles with shopping carts.

It's also important to convey to the child the fact that, good or bad, she'll always be part of the family. Some children fear that they'll be given away if they're bad, and therefore try desperately to be good. They are afraid to express anger or frustration for fear of displeasing their parents. Others may fear separation unduly, afraid that the parents will not return. One adult adoptee recalls thinking, "If I go away to camp, they may not be here when I come back. If they go away, maybe they won't come back and then who'll take care of me?"

Why did my mother give me away? Where is she now? Didn't she like me? Why should I care about her if she didn't care about me?

Many adoptive parents are very uncomfortable with these questions. Some feel threatened. Remember that for most children their close and nurturant experience has been with the adoptive family, and this is what creates attachment. These questions don't arise spontaneously before the age of seven or eight unless the parents have overemphasized adoption. With the younger child, misconceptions may arise even if they have been given accurate information, typified in the remark of one little girl, who said, "After I was borned my mother didn't like my hair so she gave me to the baby store."

The child over six understands that a child can be borne by one person and raised by another. Naturally, the responses given must vary from child to child, but an answer modeled after the following would be appropriate for a child of this age: "Another woman gave birth to you. She and your birth father wanted you but they could not take care of you because they were too young [or too poor, or had to separate, depending on the circumstances]. The doctor [or agency] helped make arrangements for us to take you home and become your parents."

"There is a special place that helps people who are not able to take care of their babies. They find people, like us, who are ready and want to be parents."

"Your birth mother was young when you were born. Maybe she was still in school and didn't have a job. She cared about you and wanted you to have a home and family. She talked to your father. They went to the adoption agency. The agency knew we wanted a baby and you came to our house. Now we're a family and we always will be."

How did my birth mother feel?

"Your birth mother must have been sad when she first decided to talk to the adoption agency. But part of her was happy because she knew that then you would always have your family and be loved. She must be a very nice person."

"Your birth parents must have felt the way that we do. We think all babies should grow up in families with parents that can look after them while they're growing up and help them when they're older. Your birth parents thought that way too, and that's why they arranged for you to be adopted."

It is important to include the idea that the birth parents loved their child and because they loved her they wanted to make sure she got the right care.

Children should hear of their birth occurring in a loving context. This is likely to contribute to positive attitudes later on toward sexuality and having babies. One adopted woman recalled: "Sometimes when I was getting ready for bed I'd ask Mom what my first mother was like. She'd say, 'She must have been a wonderful person to have had you.' Then I'd go to sleep."

Children want to believe that their birth mothers are good, and the parents' talking in terms that show regard and respect for the birth mother enhances the child's own sense of worth.

Many adoptive parents, wanting to save the child the pain of ruminating about the past, say that the birth parents died, when that is not in fact the case. But a major lie of this kind between parent and child is likely to boomerang at some later point. For example, the child may believe that in some way she was bad and therefore responsible for her parents' death. Not only that, she may then fear for the death of the adoptive parents. One six-year-old said, "You know, if you have a baby you can die, and then they give the baby away. I don't want to die or give a baby away." Another point to consider is that many adolescent and adult adoptees want to get in touch with their birth parents, and they would then uncover the lie.

Remember, the young child can't comprehend the motivations of the birth parents. In responding to the older child, however, explain the reasons why his parents gave him up (poverty, out-of-wedlock status, youth, illness) in whatever detail is known, and in a context of respect for the biological parents and their circumstances. Emphasize that the parents were concerned about the welfare of their child. Make sure to include the fact that the child was in no way responsible for the circumstances of his birth parents. Speak about the fact that the parents were not married, if that was the case. It is important that an out-of-wedlock birth remain free of degrading or immoral associations.

Feelings of sadness should be acknowledged and allowed to surface. Seven-year-old Alyse, when told of her adoption, said, "I'm sad that I didn't grow inside you. I wish I wasn't adopted." Another seven-year-old remarked, "There ought to be a law that you come out of your own mother." Convey to the child that you understand how she feels.

As children become more empathic, they are able to feel the sorrow that usually accompanies a decision to let someone else raise one's child. The child's awareness of her own feelings will be deepened if she knows her adoptive parents can recognize her sadness.

Why didn't you and Daddy [or Mommy] make your own baby? Why didn't you make me?

Telling the child before the age of six that the adoptive parents could not conceive, before she can understand the process of conception, may only imply to her that the adoptive parents may be defective in some way. But she can be told, "Well, not everybody is able to do that. Look at [list other childless couples]. Sometimes the egg and the sperm aren't able to meet in a way that will make a baby."

One father described how he explained adoption to his biological and adopted children. When the question first arose, he sent one child to the basement, one to the second floor, and one outside. He then called them all in and said, "Just as you all came in through different doors, babies can come into a family in different ways. Some are carried in Mother's uterus and some are carried in another woman's uterus and come into our family by adoption."

Even with an older child, don't emphasize infertility. This makes adoption seem like a second choice and heightens the child's feeling that he wouldn't have been adopted if his mother could have carried a child. An explanation that there are several equally positive ways to get a baby is appropriate.

The question of why the birth mother gave up the child may be turned back to the child. Many children have fantasized about this. Ask the child what she imagines. Here are some children's responses to this kind of question:

Sally, age six: "She was a nice lady who was very very poor. She had no money for food and she wore a sweater with big holes."

Gwen, 7½: "Well, I guess she just couldn't cope."

Suellen, six: "She taught school and she really loved kids and she had guinea pigs in the room. She allowed my adoption because I was too noisy."

Alex, seven: "I bet they were killed in an automobile accident."

Arthur, eight: "I guess they had too many babies already."

Who is my real family? You can't tell me what to do! You're not my real mother!

"Yes, I am. We're your real family. You didn't come from my body but we've taken care of you and that's why we're your real family, and we can tell you what to do. Even the law says we're your real family. I know you get angry with us sometimes, but that happens in every family."

Who am I? What were my grandparents like? What kind of people were they?

These are questions usually raised by adolescents. They understand what the legal process entails, what social agencies, judges, and courts are. They can empathize with others, understand the threat of poverty, the dilemma of raising a child when one is poor, or why a young person without family support might let a child be adopted. Adolescents are able to view the problems faced by their birth parents in a new perspective and may learn to regard their decision as positive. In their search for an identity and for roots, these children need more information about their birth parents. As feelings become more intense, questions increase.

Am I like my father? Was my mother tall? Do I have my mother's red hair?

An adopted girl in Jill Robinson's novel *Perdido* wonders, "How was I made? In the back of a car? In his empty dressing room? Conceived in a trailer?"

The adolescent's curiosity is apt to center on the parent of the same sex. The adopted teen-age girl, for example, trying to identify as a woman, may want to know what kind of woman her birth mother was and is, where she is, what she does, what she looks like.

Some adopted teen-agers and young adults actually go on a search for their birth parents — the media often present reports of a person's reunion with birth parents. Many adoptive parents feel they should support the child in this quest. If an agency was instrumental in the adoption, its help may be enlisted; then the child does not need to be secretive, and the birth parents can be prepared for the encounter. Some parents, however, feel threatened that their child will abandon them in her search for her birth parents. It might help to keep in mind that the child's interest stems from concern about her identity rather than from a rejection of the adoptive parents. There have been many reports that after the reunion the relationship between the child and the adoptive parents is strengthened by the realization that the adoptive parents have been the real psychological parents and that the lifelong connection is of far greater meaning than the new connection. The new relationship doesn't eradicate the old one.

In one study 95 percent of parents who had given children up for adoption indicated that they would be interested in updating the information about themselves contained in the agency case records. They wanted their children to know that they had "made it," were respected citizens in their communities, had families, were married, and, most important, that they cared about the children they had relinquished. Generally, the birth parents were grateful to the adoptive parents. Many adoption workers believe that adoptive parents should be provided with more information about the birth parents in order to help them answer their children's questions more precisely. Such information would probably decrease the amount of fantasizing that adopted children resort to in attempting to establish their identity.

The Unusual Adoption

So far we've spoken about issues that arise in the case of children adopted as infants and who are presumably of the same race as the adoptive parents. However, there are numerous other kinds of children who are adopted. Since the number of newborn white children available for adoption in the United States has been decreasing, there is now an increase in adoptions formerly considered unusual, such as the adoption of older children and children of different ethnic or racial backgrounds. Obviously, these special situations will elicit special questions from both parents and children, in addition to the questions already discussed.

The older child

> Will this be the last place?
> — eight-year-old Louis

Adoption agencies consider the child who has reached the age of five an older child. Often older children experience a conflict of loyalties between their former relationships and their new families. During the adjustment time they frequently test their new parents with questions. Many parents are actually pleased by this — as one mother said, "I thoroughly enjoy her, because she's beginning to reach out . . . to want to know answers to things." The older adopted child who is able to ask questions and talk about her memories and former emotional ties has fewer conflicts and makes a better adjustment.

How best to answer the questions? Secrecy simply isn't an option. Older children have active recollections of life before adoption. They come to their new home fully aware that they are not the natural children of the parents. When responding to the questions of a child who has lived through the breakup of her family, who has experienced a parent's illness, death, desertion, or other tragedy, it is important that the adoptive parents convey their acceptance of and respect for the child's past. Of equal importance is reassuring the child that she will always remain with her new family, that this is indeed "the last place."

Older children are preoccupied with the reasons their family relinquished or abandoned them. Answers to their questions should be handled in much the same way as discussed earlier in the chapter, but repetition and elaboration will be necessary. With children of nine or ten, it is helpful to focus on their natural parents' struggle to keep them, their reluctance to give them up, and the fact that they only let them go when their problems overwhelmed them. It was their concern for the child that caused them to seek another home for her. Children should be made aware that things were beyond the parents' control; they wanted to love and care for their child, but did not have the physical, or financial, or emotional resources and strength to do so. A positive picture of the birth parents helps children accept them, and in turn, themselves. In every child's history, there are positive aspects that may be chosen for emphasis by the adoptive parents.

It is important to let the child set the pace. Following are two reports by parents who are reacting to adopted children who have different interests and emotional needs:

> Well, she wanted to know all about her first mother, their family, her brother and sister, that sort of thing, and she wanted to know how long it would take before she could legally be our child, you know, that sort of thing. There were a lot of questions that she wanted to ask and hadn't felt free to ask before, and those were the questions she had to get all straightened out. For the first year she just talked and talked.

> We talked about being adopted and that we would go to court with the kids ... Then they both expressed a desire that they never wanted to hear anything about it again. And it has been a closed topic in our home ... If they would talk to us about it we would talk to them but as

long as they don't bring it up themselves we don't bring
it up to them.

Older children, more conscious than younger children of
having another family before the present one, may ask more
questions about their names.

*What was my name before? What was my birth mother's
name? What should I call you?*
A name is closely tied to a child's sense of identity. A
change in family name means severing old ties and making
new ones. Acceptance of the new family name symbolizes a
new stage in the identification process. The adoptive parent
would be wise not to insist that the child call him Daddy or
something similar, but merely wait and let the child come up
with what's comfortable for her. Some children do this right
away, others more slowly. Said one adolescent: "We were
never asked to call him Daddy or Father, but one day when I
saw him coming home from work, I ran to him saying, 'Hi,
Dad!' It just came naturally." Usually by the end of a year
older children stop using their former surname and start
using the adoptive parents' name; they also use a parental
name when talking to the adoptive parents.

Transracial and transcultural adoptions

These adoptions, on the increase recently, have led to con-
troversy among professionals working in the field of adoption. Some believe that no child can flourish and establish a
sense of identity and regard for her heritage if she is raised
in a family of different ethnicity or race. However, recent
studies show that several years after placement in transcul-
tural and transracial adoptive homes, children from Korea
and Vietnam are developing well, in spite of the drastic upheaval in their lives. They have made a good adjustment

when compared with children who have not undergone similar experiences. The studies show the most important factors in their adjustment to be an open attitude on the part of the adoptive parents and honest interaction within the new family. When these are strong they counterbalance other forces, such as social customs.

How best to respond to the child's questions about his or her different physical appearance from the adoptive relatives? A white parent of a black adopted boy explained, "Robbie already knows he's different from us, just by looking at the differences. We fully expect him to ask us all the questions any normal child would ask. We don't intend to keep anything from him or any of the other children. We know we can't rear him in precisely the same way a black family would, but I do know that I can give him a lot of understanding, security, love, companionship, guidance, and all of the other things that people who love and respect children pass on to them. Since I am aware of the need for every individual to know his roots and be able to relate to them, I can definitely make him aware of them." This mother seems to have incorporated into her personal philosophy the very characteristics that studies define as crucial to successful transracial adoption.

Lee Heh, a Korean, aged twelve, quoted in *Listen to Us* (the Children's Express Report):

> I used to be embarrassed to say to people that I was adopted. I guess I wanted to be like all the other kids ...
> The only different thing is that my parents don't look like me, and it's sort of weird when I introduce them. It's the same thing with my sister Holly. She looks more American 'cause she's half American. I don't think about my parents very much because I know enough of what happened to them that I'm not really curious. But if they were still alive, I'd like to go find them. A person has a right to know what her past was. The past is very impor-

tant to a person. Then you'd know more about yourself and where you came from, where you're going to, and what you were like before. I didn't go to sleep during the whole trip from Korea to America [at age seven]. My mother told me that I didn't talk the first few months. I would just listen, soak in everything. Then, after a few months, I started to talk because I really wanted to learn. I wanted to learn English so much and be like everyone else that was part of me.

As in other cases of adoption, it is important that the parents understand their own reasons for seeking this type of adoption. They will then be able to deal with the inevitable "Why did you adopt me?" when it occurs.

Children between the ages of four and seven show racial awareness, so questions such as *Why am I black and you're white?*, *Why are Song's eyes shaped like that?*, *Why is Jake's hair so curly?* will probably occur during that period. Responses that emphasize the natural acceptance of differences will help children accept their appearance and enrich their identification with their own particular heritage. Some parents, in their eagerness, may overstress the differences ("my marvelous Korean child," "my beautiful black baby") and thus run the risk of reinforcing the child's sense of feeling different, of overwhelming the child with very high expectations. The child may then feel she is responsible for the whole race or country that she comes from.

Remember, racial and cultural differences have various implications, depending on the age of the child. The young child tends to think in concrete terms. For example, Song Oak, a five-year-old adopted Korean girl, was talking to her kindergarten classmate Steven about having babies. She had been told that children are born to mothers; she had been told also that some children come into families by adoption. She also knew, from personal experience, that some children come to this country in an airplane. Using her own system of logic, she suggested to Steven that they might have some children the American way, through their mothers, and some the Korean way, by airplane.

As children grow, they become aware of the implications of their racial appearance. Many parents, adoptive and natural, want to help their children deal with racial slurs. In their book *Black Child Care* psychiatrists James Comer and Alvin Poussaint caution black parents, "if the parents' only response [to a person's slurring their child] is to tell the child to knock his block off, it might achieve the desired response, but fighting is not the best solution to the problem, even if your child wins the fights . . ." Comer and Poussaint feel parents could use racial clashes to teach their children the meaning of prejudice and to help the attacking child accept responsibility. Parents should instruct their children to view a racial slur made by a child as that child's problem of insecurity and to confront the slurrer by insisting that he or she has a problem if it's necessary to call playmates derogatory names.

For adolescents the identity crisis is compounded when they are of different background from their parents, and they will probably have more questions about natural parents, grandparents, and their place of origin. Parents would do well to make known to the older child any such information that they have.

*   *   *

Telling a child about adoption is asking for empathy on the part of the child for the parents, both biological and adoptive. No one can prescribe one answer, method, or style of communication that will be right for all parents. It is our belief that the more parents know about children at different ages, the better they can provide the help adopted children need.

6

Death

THREE-YEAR-OLD Vanessa looks sadly at a dead insect on the ground at her feet. "Is the bug sick?" she asks. If you were Vanessa's mother or father, would you respond by:

    a) taking her away from the sight of the dead insect?
    b) changing the subject?
    c) talking seriously about the philosophy of life and death?
    d) making sure she doesn't encounter dead animals again?
    e) letting her pick up the dead insect to examine it?
    f) explaining that the insect is dead and will never crawl again?
    g) telling her that the insect was naughty and is being punished?

In our culture death has replaced sex as the most taboo subject. Even sophisticated parents retreat when the subject of death arises, and children who are quite knowledgeable about the facts of life have been shielded from the facts of death.

This shielding from death wasn't possible until recently. Not so long ago, most households included several generations, so that during their growing years children often experienced the illness and death of grandparents or other older relatives. Child and infant illnesses and deaths were more frequent. Hospital care was not so common as it is today. Children learned about death as they learned about life.

Nowadays, when a death occurs in a family the children are often excluded from the funeral on the theory that it would be traumatic for them to attend. They may be sent off to relatives, showered with gifts, taken places, or protected in other ways.

"There'll be lots of time for Sarah to know about sadness. I'd like to protect her as long as I can," said one mother we interviewed. Her view is typical of many adults, who consider explanations about death threatening to children. However, totally shielding children is simply impossible, and in fact it may deny them the support of parental assurance at a time when they need it most. "Shielded" children may then feel isolated from the most important people in their life. We know from research, conversations with children, folkways, and adults' reflections on their own childhoods that death becomes part of every child's experience whether we like it or not. Often the death of a pet is a child's first awareness of mortality. Child analyst Selma Fraiberg, author of *The Magic Years,* relates the following story in her book:

> Early one morning I received a phone call from the mother of a five year old boy. "I'm calling from upstairs so Greg won't hear this. Ernest died this morning. What shall I tell Greg?" "How terrible" I said, "but who is Ernest?" "Ernest is Greg's hamster" she said. "This will break his heart. I don't know how to tell him. Bill is going to stop off at the pet shop on his way home from work tonight and pick up a new hamster, but I just dread breaking the news to Greg. Please tell me what to say to him?" "Why don't you tell him that his hamster died?" "Died" said my friend, shrinking at my crudity.

"What I want to know is how I can break the news gently
to him and spare him the pain of this whole experience.
I thought I would tell him that Ernest went to heaven.
Would that be all right to tell him?" "Only if you're sure
that Ernest went to heaven" I said in my best consulting
room voice. "Oh stop" my friend begged "this is very
serious. I don't mean the hamster. I mean this is Greg's
first experience with death. I don't want him to be hurt."
"All right" I said. "What right do we have to deprive
Greg of his feelings? Why isn't he entitled to grieve over
the death of his pet? Why can't he cry and feel the full
measure of pain that comes with the discovery that death
is an end and that Ernest is no more?"

Children identify with their pets and transfer feelings to
them as if they were human. The death of a loved pet causes
shock; the experience is a profound one. What does a quick
replacement of a dead hamster by a new live one suggest to
the child? That everyone can be replaced? That there is no
difference between the animate and the inanimate? That all
pets, and perhaps all people, are alike and that the special
feelings a child may have experienced for her pet, or for a
friend or relative, are trivial and easily transferable from one
to another? Margaret Mead, the anthropologist, felt that giving children the opportunity to care for animals enabled
them to have contact with the cycle of life, including death.
Particularly important, she noted, was experience with life
in this era of lifeless and mechanical toys.

Actually, mourning is similar to loving. Both are deep,
meaningful emotions, and without them the quality of our
lives, religion, literature, and art would be superficial and
mechanistic.

It's not our aim to induce guilt in parents who, in their
desire to protect their children from sadness, have offered
them a quick resurrection and replacement of a dead pet. If
the quality of the interpersonal relationships in the home is

good, obviously a single remark or act will not convey to the child the impression that all of us are exchangeable for new models. But bear in mind that death, whether of a pet, a playmate, a neighbor, or a public figure, intrudes on every child's life. Moreover, one child in twenty loses a parent during childhood. It is not really possible to protect children from this reality.

Should you need further convincing that experiences with separation, illness, and death are inevitable, we cite a study conducted by the staff of the Center for Preventive Psychiatry in White Plains, New York. The following events were recorded in the lives of a group of sixteen ordinary nursery-school children during a two-week period: a tonsillectomy, the death of a relative in a car crash, the sudden hospitalization of a sister in the middle of the night, a brother's operation, the death of a grandmother, the death of a turtle, the death of a cat, the death of an aunt, a hernia operation on a cousin, and the revelation that an uncle had died the preceding month. Considering the number of such events, it is unrealistic to believe that children can avoid thinking about death. Moreover, TV news seems to bring at least one death a minute.

Despite the universality of the experience, there is remarkably little communication in most families regarding death. In a survey conducted by *Psychology Today* in 1971, one-third of the respondents could not recall from childhood a single discussion of death within their family circle. One adult remembered, "When I was twelve, my mother died of leukemia. When I woke up, my parents were gone. My father came home, took me on his knee, burst into screeching sobs, and said, 'Jesus took your mother.' Then we never talked about it again."

Why is it so difficult to know what to say to children? Are we afraid of upsetting them? Or are we ourselves afraid? Most of the time we pretend that the threat of old age and death does not exist. We lapse into a silence and try to reassure our-selves that all is well and that life will continue as it has done up to now, that we shall neither get old nor die.

In a recent study of children's fears conducted by E. A. Lazar for the National Institute of Health, it was found that 80 percent of their fears were about death, but that children's death fears are different from adults'.

Unlike adults, children are not primarily afraid of growing old and dying; they're most afraid of being separated from their parents, losing them, or losing their love and protection.

Through the combination of lack of information from parents, easy access to television and other media, and wish fulfilling magical thinking typical of young children, misconceptions about death are common.

What can parents do? When we speak to our children about death, it's important to know what they understand, what thought processes they're capable of, and what the typical fears, fantasies, and misconceptions of their particular age are. If we can tailor our explanations to the children's needs, we can help them acquire reasonable ideas about death and avoid confusion and frightening fantasies. And, most crucial, we can help them deal with their distress when they are faced with the reality of death, as well as aid them in mourning. The child's experiences of sadness and grief are necessary, even if they're heartbreaking for the adult to watch.

Let's consider the child's developing abilities.

Intellectual Development
Before the Age of Three

Little understanding of death is apparent at this time, al-though infants do fear separation beginning at about eight months. As toddlers develop curiosity and explore their environment, they become interested in where things go and disappearance: simple early childhood games such as peekaboo (which stems from Old English words meaning "alive or dead?"), all-gone, blowing out matches, and hiding and finding things appeal to the child's interest in games of disappearance and reappearance. Robert Kastenbaum, a psychologist who has investigated children's ideas about death, writes about his eighteen-month-old son, who placed a dead bird on a tree and tried to explain to his father that it would fly again. A week later the child insisted that autumn leaves be raked up and replaced on the tree.

Between the Ages of Three and Five

Children at these ages ask questions about the concrete details of the funeral, the coffin, the cemetery, and so forth, as they try to understand and master the ideas surrounding death — to gain a sense of control. However, certain characteristics of children's thinking at this time preclude a true understanding of the nature of death, which is an abstract and complex idea.

Children's thinking at this age is concrete and animistic. Not quite sure what the words *dead* and *alive* mean, most preschoolers regard life and death as related to mobility: moving means life; lack of movement means death. Many children do not believe that plants are alive, because they don't move. If you're playing dead, you lie still; if you get up, you're alive again. Therefore, clouds, cars, and trains are viewed as alive, whereas trees are not.

When we asked preschool children what the word *dead* meant, they said, "You can't walk or play the piano anymore," or "You go to the hospital," or "You go to the angels." So we can understand why they may be confused by adult phrases such as "live wire," "dead end," and "deadhead."

Their literal interpretation of language leads to many mis-conceptions. Four-year-old Alicia, on hearing that her grand-mother's dead body was being shipped from Florida, wanted to know whether her head was being shipped, too. Similarly, the phrase "going to the doctor for a shot" may sound quite ominous to the child.

The young child's limited sense of time also prevents un-derstanding of death. Children cannot comprehend that there may have been a time when they did not exist. Four-year-old Cindy was shown a picture of her parents and told that it was taken on their honeymoon before she was born. "But where am I?" she asked. When told that she had not yet been born, she burst into tears and asked if she were dead. The answer "You were inside Mommy" satisfied her; the fear of being separated from her parents had overwhelmed her. Five-year-old Mark: "My grandma died last year. I didn't know she was going to stay dead so long."

Many children at this age view death as a reduced level of life — the dead are simply somewhat less alive. There are degrees of being dead. The dead cannot see or hear very well; they're not as hungry as the living. Some believe that the dead can hear ("he can hear the leaves falling on the grave"). Others believe the dead can think ("she would like to come out but the coffin is nailed down"). They believe that the dead can feel smothered and cold, or are asleep ("does she have a blanket and sheets in there?"). One little girl was ob-served practicing writing the word *Nana* upside down. When asked what she was doing she replied, "So Nana can read it from up in heaven." The actress Liv Ullmann in her book *Changing* writes of her reaction to the loss of her father when she was under the age of six: "One day I buried all my dolls at his grave. I didn't want him to lie there alone. I stole flowers from other graves to brighten up the place for Papa and the dolls."

Death in the mind of the preschooler is accidental, rather

than inevitable; one dies under certain conditions, which may or may not occur. "If you get runned over, then you be dead" or "He's old, he's dead." If you don't get run over or old you won't die. The accompanying assumption is that they themselves will not die, since they are not old or sick — in young children's thinking, not everyone necessarily encounters death. A wise five-year-old, out to protect herself, said, "Somebody will have to bury the last person, so I'll do it." "I won't die 'cause my mother doesn't want me to," said one confident preschooler.

Death is not perceived as a final event. The idea that it's reversible can be observed in many of the games that children play. Although they use words such as *bang-bang, killing, dead,* and *shooting,* it's unlikely that the words are employed in the true sense. To the young, being dead is a temporary state: "I won't kill you bad," promises one child. Said another, "I'll kill you when I put the knife in, but when I take the knife out you won't be dead anymore." A bad person can be shot and then be alive again. It's like taking a trip and then returning.

For some children, ritual provides a way to express and act out concerns. Ring-around-a-rosy is said to have originated during the time of the Black Death. If adults had no control over the plague, what could children do? They chanted ritualistically, moving in a reassuring rhythm of unity, and then *they* decided when they would "all fall down!" This was a playing at death with one distinct advantage — one could rise again.

Much in our environment encourages this idea of the temporariness of death. When a person on a television show dies, he can be seen again the next week; people are said to be residing up in heaven; we speak of Christ rising from the dead. Adults tell ghost stories, talk about an afterlife, and often use euphemisms, such as "Aunt Sophie's with the angels," "Joe went to sleep for a long time," or "Cousin Abe has passed on," all of which, rather than softening the idea of death for children, lend themselves to inaccurate if not frightening interpretations.

These are four-year-old Miranda's views of the comings and goings of animals and people between the earth and heaven:

MIRANDA: This bird of my friend, he's only a little baby but he's dead already.
INTERVIEWER: Will you ever see him again?
MIRANDA: No, 'cause I can't go up there, but if I die I can see him.
INTERVIEWER: Do you think he'll come back?
MIRANDA: Yes, he'll come down from heaven. He could fly.
INTERVIEWER: Do people die or just birds?
MIRANDA: Birds and people. Someone's a cop, right, they get shooted by a robber. Then they get up in heaven with everybody else.
INTERVIEWER: Do you see him again? Do they come back from heaven?
MIRANDA: Birds could fly but people, no, they don't have wings.
INTERVIEWER: Birds fly down from heaven then?
MIRANDA: Yes.
INTERVIEWER: But how about the cop?
MIRANDA: He don't have no wings.

In a similar vein, Edward, age four, said in a disappointed tone, "When I flew on the airplane, I looked on every cloud for Skipper [his dog], but I couldn't see him."

In a study conducted by psychologist Gerald Koocher, children were asked, "How do you make dead things come back to life?" The answer: "Keep them warm and give them hot food," implying that death need not be permanent if somebody takes proper care of the corpse. The writer Frieda Lawrence speaks of an early memory of finding her guinea pigs dead of frost: "We covered them on a tray with leaves and put them in the oven."

This statement by a four-year-old girl to her eighty-four-year-old great-grandmother illustrates the preschooler's ideas about death: "You're old. That means you're going to die. I'm young so I won't die, you know." A few minutes later she added, "But it's all right. Just make sure you wear your white dress so after you die you can marry Poppa [the great-grandfather] again and have babies."

Six to Nine Years

At about six years of age many children become fascinated with killing: "I'll kill you dead!" "I'll chop you to pieces!" Some six-year-olds may also become interested in rituals and be disturbed by pictures and stories of dying and dead animals, but they still don't believe that they themselves will die. In the minds of some children death is personified, seen as a separate person, an angel or bogeyman who appears in the night to take people away. Researcher Maria Nagy, who studied the ideas about death of about 400 children between the ages of three and ten, quotes a nine-year-old: "Death is very dangerous. You never know what minute he is going to carry you off with him. Death is invisible, something nobody has ever seen in all the world. But at night he comes to everybody and carries them off with him. Death is like a skeleton. All the parts are made of bone. But then when it begins to be light, when it's morning, there's not a trace of him. It's that dangerous, death." But the child of this age still feels death may be eluded, outwitted, and does not believe it to be universal. This allows an important protective device to operate: if you run faster than the bogeyman, or trick him, then you won't die.

At about eight years old, children become interested in

what happens after death and ask numerous questions about the disposition of the body, a subject that many adults would prefer to be silent about. The child who can now understand the meaning of time realizes that this separation differs not only in degree but in kind from the previous ones: it is forever.

By nine or ten children understand that death is universal, inevitable, final, and personal. They come to realize that their parents will die one day and so will they. They can accurately distinguish between animate and inanimate objects, and can conceive of death as a permanent biological process. For some children the new awareness is accompanied by a belief in a form of afterlife. As one nine-year-old said, "Everyone has to die once, but the soul lives on." In fact, the very concept of afterlife is dependent on comprehending the finality of physical death.

*   *   *

No matter what their stage of intellectual development, children's understanding of death is interwoven with their emotional reactions to it. Before infants learn to distinguish themselves from other people and one person from another, a loss has little or no impact and they accept a substitute mother readily. After infancy, however, children experience close relationships and then, despite the difficulty in understanding death, they are profoundly influenced by a loss. A severe emotional reaction is possible even in the absence of the intellectual equipment necessary to comprehend the experience. In fact, the very absence of intellectual comprehension intensifies the shattering impact of death on younger children. They are unable to reflect on it, to allay their fears, to reassure themselves that although one person has left, others remain, and they will continue to be loved and cared for.

A child's age is of crucial importance in determining how

traumatic the loss is. The psychoanalyst Humberto Nagera has written extensively on children's reactions to death at different levels of emotional development. The child's need for the parents differs from one developmental stage to another. According to Nagera, in the early years the loss of a mother is more devastating than that of a father. Later on, during the oedipal and adolescent years, the father's role becomes significant and his absence or loss is equally shattering.

Emotional Development
The Child to Age Six

Nagera feels that it is natural and normal for the younger child to deny that the death has occurred ("she'll be here in time for the vacation"). He observed the reaction of one four-year-old to the death of her father: the child was told about it and seemed to accept his absence; nevertheless, several months later, on her birthday, she was distressed because her father didn't come to her party or send her any presents.

About the age of four, children believe in the omnipotence of their parents, an idea that precludes the possibility that they may die. Nagera quotes four-year-old Peter, who, when told that his father was killed in the war and that he couldn't come home, said, "I want him to come. My Daddy is big; he can do anything."

Some young children may acknowledge the loss but secretly put food out for the missing person. Some children's mood may revert to its opposite; they may laugh, not cry — "I don't mind that Mommy died. I can watch TV." They may become anxious about any separation, may search for substitutes for the lost person, or may become fearful that they, too, will die or that other important people will die.

The quality of the children's relationship to their parents

of course influences their reactions to the death of a parent; in addition, young children's inability to distinguish between reality and fantasy can complicate their feelings. All children are at times angry with their parents and wish for their disappearance and replacement by a better set: a child may say, "Amy's parents aren't mean like you. I wish you were dead and I could live with Amy's parents!" Because young children cannot distinguish between the wish and the deed, when death does in fact occur they may feel they were responsible for it, that somehow their wishes had magically caused the death. An adult woman recalls: "In many ways I hated my mother for being sick. When she did die, I thought it was because I wished it so. Years later I still avoided closeness, because, like a black widow, I had the power to kill and the feeling that I would surely always lose those I cared for through death."

Children whose wishes are "fulfilled" may be consumed with feelings of guilt and/or fear of retribution. They may also feel guilty because they think they didn't take good care of the lost person, a feeling that many adults have after the death of someone close. "Is it my fault that Granny died?" asked one six-year-old; "I didn't carry her packages up the steps." Five-year-old Annie thought she was responsible for her mother's death, because she made so much noise after she had been asked to play quietly. "Did Mommy catch my cold?" asked another anxious six-year-old.

Seven to Nine Years

Many of the same factors play a role in the reactions to death of the child from seven to nine. Even though children of these ages have reached a level of abstract thinking, there are still areas in which concreteness lingers or returns. This is particularly true during times of stress or anxiety. Although the behavior of older children may give the impression that they are dealing with the loss, they may be suffering inwardly. Typically there is denial or a reversal of the emotions deemed appropriate by adults. Even when children are old enough to mourn, they may lack the capacity to sustain the sad mood. Martha Wolfenstein, a child psychoanalyst, refers to the "short sadness span which is usual in children," and cites as examples children aged nine or ten who cried when they heard the news of John Kennedy's assassination and yet could not understand why their parents refused to go to the movies that night.

Seven to nine years is when children deny death by joking and playing games. Most of us can remember rhymes and chants about sickness and death — "The worms crawl in, the worms crawl out, a nice fat juicy one right in your mouth." Iona Opie and Peter Opie, in *The Lore and Language of Schoolchildren,* collected the jokes and games of English children, including, typically, "It's not the cough that carries you off, it's the coffin they carry you off in." Halloween, with its spooks, witches, and scary stories, offers children a ritualized way of taunting evil spirits and thoughts of death.

General Guidelines

1. *Tell the truth.* Children can understand sadness better than deception or evasion. When there is a death in the family, tell the children the facts according to their age and emotional needs. Ten-year-old Mary resentfully recalled, "I loved my grandfather. When he died nobody told me. I saw my mother crying but I didn't know why. When I found out he died I locked myself in my room and wouldn't let anybody in. I wasn't crying only because my grandfather died, but also because nobody told me."

2. *Be simple and direct.* For young children the best ex-

planations are those that draw on concrete experiences. They learn that flowers die, they see a dead insect or pet. Dying and death have been shown in movies and on television, and there have been several sensitive books about death written for children of different ages. All these treatments offer opportunities for discussion. It's also a good idea to have the children explain in their own words what they have been told. In this way, any gross distortions can be corrected on the spot. An example of the way in which a young child can link ideas together erroneously is cited by the psychologist Len Chaloner, whose daughter once watched him kill a bug. "I got him! I killed him! He won't bother us anymore!" announced Chaloner triumphantly. Sometime later the little girl asked where her grandmother was. "She's dead" was the reply. "Who killed her?" was the next question.

To older children the real cause of death should be explained, to forestall concerns about their own health and future. But if the child doesn't ask, don't go into graphic detail about what happens after death.

3. *Don't hide your grief.* Even children who can't grasp the actual facts can grasp the emotional reality. This may be the first time they see adults cry, and it should be explained that all people cry when they feel sad. Child psychologist Haim Ginott helped one child by saying to him, "Do you know what your tears tell me? They tell me you're growing up and you can really feel deeply."

4. *Keep the child with the family if at all possible.* Familiar surroundings and routines provide security and a sense that things will go on. Children over five or six are usually sufficiently mature to attend a funeral if they wish to. This helps them know in the most concrete way possible what happens to the body. "What I want to know is how will he get out of that box?" asked one incredulous little boy. The simple act of placing a flower or throwing a handful of dirt into the grave enables children to participate with the family

in a meaningful ritual and to sense the importance of the event.

5. *Encourage the child to talk and ask questions.* Don't assume that children react in the way that you do; they may be upset, if, for example, you provide more information than they want at that moment. Accept the child's reaction, no matter what it is, or, more difficult still, accept a lack of reaction; the reaction may be delayed or it may not last. Help children express grief openly, and acknowledge anger — let them know it's O.K. to feel mad. Five-year-old Sandy: "Why did Daddy die?" "It must be God's will," answered his mother. "I hate God," he said.

Listen to what the children are really saying, not only to their words. Try to find out the meanings they attach to death. What are their thoughts, associations, and feelings? What do they really want to know from you? Do they need reassurance about your continued existence? Do separation and death mean the same thing to them? Their questions and concerns are not going to be immediately obvious but rather are more likely to emerge gradually over a period of time. It's wise to try and maintain a continuing dialogue; all the information doesn't have to be transmitted in one discussion.

If their questions to parents are respected at the time they arise, children won't have to turn to others or fill in the gaps with their imagination. Slowly they will gain an understanding of death and deal with the grief. Let the sorrow run its course.

6. *Expect some unusual behavior.* Children's concerns may be expressed in such nonverbal ways as a change in sleeping or eating habits and in relationships with other children or relatives. Some children react in a way that to adults seems nonfeeling. In protecting themselves against sadness children may eat greedily, do forbidden things, or act out their feelings in other ways. Their school work may slip. If they feel guilty they may deliberately do things that result in punishment.

Make sure your children realize that the death was in no way connected with their behavior.

7. *Try to explore your own feelings about death.* What are your explanations for yourself? Who really understands death? There's no one way to answer the questions of a child. Whatever way is comfortable for you is the best way. Your explanation may be religious; it may be scientific; it may focus on the values of life and death in general. Don't use a religious explanation if you don't believe it yourself; it simply won't ring true and your child will know it.

What is most crucial when your child has lost someone is to communicate your availability. Children must know that you understand what is happening to them. They may wish to talk about experiences they have shared with the dead person or about their anxious feelings. Discussing familiar things is a way of reinforcing the stability and continuity of life's routine. Nonverbal communication — holding or hugging your children — will indicate that they can count on you for support. Let them express their sadness and listen to them.

8. Here are some expressions to avoid in general conversation with children:

"You'll be the death of me."

"Drop dead."

"I'll murder you."

"I'll kill myself if you get left back in school."

"I'll die of shame if you don't go to Sunday school."

"You're making me sick."

"You'll catch your death of cold."

And some expressions to avoid when someone dies:

"She died of a broken heart."

"Mommy has gone on a long trip" or "Mommy has left us."

"God took her, because he wants the good people in heaven."

"Grandpa's been put to rest," or "Susie passed away," or "Mike is sleeping."

"Be brave. Brave children don't cry."

These are the kinds of remarks that cause children, in their literal way, to form misconceptions. They may be terrified by the figures of speech; they may fantasize about Mommy's return; they may think they'll go next, since good people all go to heaven; they may worry about going on trips, sleeping, or lying down to take a rest. And of course, children must be allowed — encouraged — to express their grief by crying.

Questions Commonly Asked by Preschool Children

(All the responses should be accompanied by an acknowledgment of feelings, verbally or non-verbally.)

About the deaths of animals or plants

What does that mean, "the bird is dead"?

"It means that he can't move anymore. His body is stiff. He won't be able to fly." (Allow the child to hold the dead animal and feel it if she wants to.)

Who deaded him?

"Nobody. He died by himself."

If you kill the bird just at the very, very tip of his wing, will he die?

"Yes, he will. All of him will be dead."

Why do we bury the bird?

"So the body won't just be around and get stepped on or run over or something like that. It can't move anymore."

Will the bird get fixed when it's buried?

"No, the bird is dead and can't get fixed anymore."

What happens to the bird under the ground?

"The bird can't see or fly, and his body will become part of the earth. You're alive and you probably feel sorry that birds die." (The child attributes emotions and functions similar to his own to the bird and may think the bird will get

lonely, scared of the dark, hungry, or be unable to breathe.)
When is a tree dead?
"When it has no leaves and its bark is falling off and it can't grow anymore."
If we bury Skippy in the yard, will he come back when the flowers grow?
"No, Skippy is dead. That means he won't come back."

About the deaths of children

What happens to Paul when it rains? Does he get wet? Can he come home when it rains?
"He can't come home, but the rain or snow or cold can't hurt him or bother him anymore. I guess you think about him a lot. I do, too. We all miss him very much."
What will happen to the baby? Who will change his diaper and give him his bottle?
"The baby can't move or wet his diaper or drink his bottle. I'm very sad about that and I think you're feeling sad, too. We both wish he hadn't died and we're feeling lonely."
Can he still have a birthday party when he's dead?
"No, you can't have parties when you've died."

About heaven as a concrete place

What happens to the people in heaven when it thunders? If Grandpa went to heaven, how come we put him in the ground? How come heaven doesn't fall down when there are so many people up there? If I die when I'm on my bike, can I ride it to heaven? How will I know Scotty when I get to heaven? Are the angels watching the baby? Does it take a long time to get to heaven?

Religion can comfort people and offer an acceptable explanation of death to children. This is a personal matter and you should make use of whatever religious beliefs you have. You may wish to explain your own belief in life after death, but it is important to make clear to the child that the physical body ceases to live and grow after death. The Reverend Edgar Jackson, who has served as chairman of the Mental Health Board of the New York Methodist Conference, suggests the following explanation if it conforms with your beliefs: "Grandpa became old and his body did not suit him any more so he moved out of it. His body had aches and pains and he was uncomfortable in it. Grandpa still exists but he doesn't live in his body any more."

If you do not believe that souls go to heaven, simply say that there is no real place called heaven, but some people like to imagine it or that we're still trying to find out about it. You can say that we don't know what happens to a person after death; what is important is how one lives.

About the cause of death and feelings of guilt

Will she come back if I'm good? I should have given Tom my bike. Then he wouldn't have died, would he? Did Mommy die because I didn't like spaghetti?

"That's not why Mommy died. She died because she was very, very sick. Nothing you did made her die. She won't come back, but we can always think about her. I'm very sad and I know you're sad, too."

Why didn't the doctor make her better?

"Most of the time doctors help sick people get better. But sometimes a person can have a very bad sickness and nothing at all can make her or him better."

About death as a reduced form of life

Do you keep growing in heaven? What does a person say when he dies? How do you go to the bathroom when you're

*dead? How does he get out of the box? Do you have feelings
when you're dead?*

"A dead person can't grow and can't talk and can't see and
can't hear and can't go to the bathroom and can't get out of
the box. A dead person doesn't have any feelings."

When do dead people wake up again?

"Dead people don't wake up again."

Will Susannah fall to pieces like the flowers?

"A body does fall to pieces like flowers. But we're alive
and we can always think about Susannah and keep her in our
minds."

About fears that others will die

Are you going to die, too?

"I'm probably going to live until you're old. I take good
care of myself. When I'm sick I go to the doctor so she can
help me get well. Don't worry, there'll always be somebody
to take care of you. We're all going to go on living together
for a very long time."

Can little children die, too?

"Most children live until they're very old. Once in a while
a child may die, but it doesn't happen very often, only from
an extra-bad sickness or because of an accident."

*If you're sleeping can somebody think you're dead and bury
you by accident?*

"No, we can tell the difference between sleeping and
dying. Sleeping is not dying. Nobody gets buried by accident."

Questions Commonly Asked by the Child of Six to Nine

What happens to the body?

"Dead people are buried in special places called cemeteries.
Stones are put on each grave to tell the names of the people.

The place is kept beautiful with flowers and trees. It's a pleasant place to visit and helps us remember the person who died. Before people are buried, there's often a funeral. This is a way that people can say good-by forever to someone they care about."

Why do they bury dead people?

"Because dead bodies don't smell good after a short time and burying them helps them gradually to become part of the earth. The particles of the body will finally be distributed into soil, air, and water."

Why did he die?

The older child should be told the facts about the death — the person was old, had a bad sickness, was hurt in an automobile accident, whatever the case may be.

Why did it have to happen to him?

"I wish I knew the answer to that. We can cure a lot of sicknesses but there are still some we don't know how to cure." Or, "No matter how careful we are, there are still some accidents we can't help."

Do people live in another world after they die?

"We still don't know that. People are trying to find out, just as they're trying to find out about outer space. Probably when you're grown up you'll go on trying to find out, too." (This response will depend on your beliefs.)

Could I have stopped him from dying?

"We all took the very best care of him that we could. We did the best we could do at the time. You've always been a fine and good daughter, and I know your father loved you. Even when he scolded you or yelled at you, he loved you. There's nothing you could have done that would have stopped him from dying."

Who will take care of us? Will there be money for food?

"My health is fine. I'll take care of you. We'll have money for food and for clothes and for a place to live."

If you yourself are worried about these specific things,

don't reassure your children falsely, but rather stress that the family will be together and they'll always be taken care of.

* * *

The following incident related by Marjorie Mitchell, a teacher, occurred in a classroom occupied by seven-year-olds who had found a dead bird outside their window. The children asked their teacher if they could have a funeral.

ROSA: We must bury it. We can use our garden.

JOHN: Let's get a box for it.

The bird in its box was carried in slow procession, followed by about ten boys and girls, and laid on the ground while John dug a grave.

ANGELA: We ought to put flowers on its coffin.

JOHN: It's got blue on its wings. It should have blue flowers.

Meanwhile, an argument had started.

ROSA: The coffin should have a cover. You have to nail a coffin down.

JILL: No, it's awful to have a cover. It's awful to be shut up.

JOHN: Don't be silly. It's dead, isn't it?

ROSA: How would you like to be buried in a coffin with no cover and all that dirt all over your face?

JILL: I wouldn't care at all. You're silly.

PETER: I think we ought to have a cross. You should have a cross on a grave.

ROSA: Ask Paul to make one. He's doing woodwork.

Paul agreed, but came back later saying, "Robert doesn't think it should have a cross. It might be a Jewish bird."

The rest agreed except for John, who said they were crazy and he had finished digging. By now the children with the flowers returned and arranged them around the bird. They covered the coffin and without further protests the coffin was placed in the earth and covered over by John. An uneasy silence was broken by Rosa, who said, "You sing something at funerals."

At this point the bell rang for classes. One of the children then came up to the teacher and said, "I wonder if there is a part of the bird that comes out invisible and flies away. If I came back from my recorder lesson and heard that bird chirping again, I'd drop my recorder and jump all over the place."

He was the only child who verbalized his feelings about the death of the bird.

7

Crime and Punishment

"WHEN YOU eat with your fingers, you don't get into trouble, but when you steal you do."

"It's not right to eat with your fingers, but your parents wouldn't call in the cops if you did, not even if you ate spaghetti with your fingers. But if you steal something from somebody's house, they would call the cops and you could get put in jail."

These children were asked to compare the infraction of a social convention — eating with one's fingers — with the breaking of a moral law — stealing. Whether we're aware of it or not, we begin to teach both social conventions and moral rules early in life. The children quoted above participated in a study conducted by William Damon of Clark University, who was interested in determining how early children were capable of making this distinction. Damon found that children's views changed with their ages: One-third of the children between the ages of four and five thought stealing worse. Two-thirds of the six-year-olds thought stealing worse. Almost all of the seven- and eight-year-olds thought stealing worse.

Early in life most children learn that they can't take what appeals to them unless they have permission from the owner or money to pay for it. But merely learning the rules doesn't guarantee that the child won't steal. Information from the official FBI crime statistics for 1977 shows a breakdown according to age of arrests of children: in that year, in cities only, almost 68,000 children under the age of ten, 136,000 eleven- and twelve-year-olds, and 417,000 thirteen- and fourteen-year-olds were arrested.

"Property crime" was the most frequent offense. These statistics cover only actual arrests and probably include only those children whose stealing had become a pattern. Most occasional stealing by children is confined to shoplifting, which often goes undetected and does not result in an arrest. Should the child be caught stealing in a store, the policy followed by most stores is that the police are not notified but the child is told never to come to the store again. The parents may be called and disciplinary action left to them after the store is reimbursed for the stolen items.

It could happen in your family. One day your child may come home with bubble gum, chocolate bars, or a matchbox car, none of which he has paid for. Or he will "borrow" crayons from school. Or he may "borrow" a dollar from your wallet while you're out of the room. Is he on his way to a life of crime? Is his action evidence of poor moral character? And when he asks, "Why can't I keep the bubble gum [or crayons, or money]?," what will you say after you say, "Certainly not!"

Whether your child was consciously stealing depends of course on his age and understanding of the rules against stealing. As soon as children are old enough to go shopping with their parents, they are constantly tempted by alluring things openly displayed on reachable counters. Since you're probably not always willing or able to buy whatever they request, children may take matters into their own hands — literally. They don't know much about private property, and you may talk to them about waiting for a birthday or Christ-

mas, but the younger they are the harder it is for them to wait
for future gratifications. When the very young child takes
something, it can't be considered stealing. Apologize to the
owner or salesperson and replace what was taken. Toddlers
don't ask why they can't keep the things they took; they do
learn from your tone and from your actions that taking things
without permission or without giving money in exchange for
them is frowned upon.

What do we know about children's ideas of stealing? Age
is a most important factor. The child under four thinks of
good and bad, right and wrong, not in moral terms but rather
in relation to consequences: "That boy was bad," remarked
four-year-old Dana. "How do you know?" asked her father.
"Because he got punished," was her response. Even with five-
and six-year-olds, cause and effect sometimes get mixed up;
how grave the misdeed was is judged by the consequences
rather than by the misdoer's intent, as illustrated in the following interviews. The interviewer told a six-year-old and
an eight-year-old a story, and the children's responses distinguish the typical thinking of these two ages:

"Two boys did some things they shouldn't have done. Listen to the story and then I'll ask you which boy was naughtier.
The first boy was told not to eat candy, but he climbed up on
the kitchen cabinets to get some candy he knew was up there.
While he was climbing up, he broke one cup. The second boy
was helping to set the table for dinner. While he was setting
the table, he broke ten cups by accident. Which boy was
naughtier?"

Fred, six: "The one who broke the ten cups, because
they're supposed to be on the dinner table for all the family,
and he broke 'em, and that was the worst thing he did. The
other one did bad too, but he broke one cup only." Fred
thinks that the more damage is done, the more severe is the
crime. The intent underlying the action doesn't interest him.

Maureen, eight: "The one climbing up on the cabinet was

worse, because the other boy was helping and by accident he broke them, and the other boy was climbing and his mother told him not to. The one who was trying to help, he broke ten, but he was trying to help." Obviously, Maureen is mature enough to take intent into account.

Six-year-olds don't have the intellectual equipment to appreciate concepts such as the golden rule; they're usually more worried about punishment than concerned for the welfare of others.

At about seven or eight, children usually develop the "law-and-order" orientation. They believe that good behavior consists of doing one's duty, showing respect for authority, and conforming to the social order. Intellectually mature adolescents and adults are capable of criticizing established rules that they view as unjust. For example, war resisters and civil-rights activists oppose government policies that clash with their own ethical principles; they follow their conscience and act to bring about justice, ready to accept punishment for their actions.

If we bear in mind that understanding rules depends on the child's level of intellectual development, it follows that stealing has different meanings for different ages; it also can represent more than simply the desire to possess something. The very young, who don't really understand what rules are, should not be punished for taking something, although they must be told not to. When the child does begin to understand the rules, stealing may be experimentation or a provocation of the parents. With teen-agers, who are fully capable of understanding rules, stealing may become a group activity, a response to peer pressure, a sport, an expression of rebellion against authority — the possibility of getting caught is exciting.

Stealing can have many personal meanings. Sometimes it is the only way a child can overcome a sense of worthlessness or depression. Stealing can be a way of acquiring something that makes you feel good. Sometimes children steal money to buy candy or other objects to bribe other children to play with them. Some may steal to express their hostility. To children who feel deprived of affection the stolen object may represent love. To others it's a revolt against an authoritarian parent. Many older children steal from time to time, but the child who steals compulsively and repeatedly reveals deep emotional problems, which must be dealt with.

Children can be aware of the various reasons for stealing. The deprivation motivation is articulated by Steffi, age eleven: "It could be that kids are insecure. Maybe if they had more people caring for them, they wouldn't do it. Instead of having a big fit, the parents should try to talk to them."

Martin, twelve: "Some people steal just for the fun of it or to go along with the crowd. When they don't have any money, they decide to get something for free and they steal something. I know a lot of people who do it. They check their pockets, 'I'm broke,' and they zip into the store and steal. When I take something, I always feel bad. It gives a temptation, something that's just laying there. I feel like grabbin' it and runnin' out of the store. The only thing is, after I take something, which is very seldom, I feel all guilty and I don't usually go to the same store afterwards . . ."

Stealing in groups is fairly common. Psychologist Edward Diener and his associates at the University of Illinois investigated the conditions under which children will steal. On Halloween Diener placed experimenters in a number of houses to observe trick-or-treating children; the experimenters' task was to tempt the children and to see whether they succumbed to or resisted temptation. When the children arrived, they were greeted by an experimenter playing the role of the inhabitant of the house. She showed the children two bowls on a table, one with candy and one with money, and told them, "You [or, each of you] may take *one* of the candies. I have to go back to my work in another room."

Some of the children were asked their names and others were permitted to remain anonymous; in the case of groups of anonymous children, the experimenter sometimes appointed a leader. When the experimenter left the room, an assistant observed the children through a peephole. Diener and associates found that stealing occurred mostly among children who were permitted to remain anonymous, easy to do since they wore costumes and masks. In addition, stealing was more apt to occur when the anonymous children had arrived at the houses in groups rather than individually, and its most frequent occurrence was among groups of anonymous children for whom the experimenter had appointed a leader (also anonymous); it seems that the leader was viewed by the others as being responsible for their behavior, even though none of the children could be identified.

Based on this study, Diener and his associates suggest that rules against stealing are easily violated when people are viewed not as individuals, but only as anonymous members of groups. Shoplifting indeed occurs most frequently among children in groups in cities, where anonymity is easy.

The Parents' Role
What you can do

Few children ask specific questions about stealing, other than why can't they keep their loot. But parents must respond firmly to stealing: the implicit questions posed by children's behavior should be answered not only in words but also in action. Action, of course, includes the example set by the parents.

There are some parents whose behavior communicates to their children that they may break rules as long as they don't get caught; some who give a double message — that breaking rules is O.K. sometimes; and a few parents whose behavior actively encourages rule breaking.

Pam, eleven: "If the parents steal sometimes, then the kids are going to do it, too."

Jack, eight: "I sneak on the bus a lot. My mother wants me to because she doesn't have the change. It always works, and the bus driver never pays attention. A lot of other people do it, too. It usually works when it's rush hour and the buses are packed."

To help your children learn that stealing is wrong, review your own behavior. In addition, minimize temptations around the house; don't leave lots of accessible cash around. Other family habits may need revision. If a child asks for money and is told to take it from his father's or mother's wallet, or if a child is used to seeing one parent going through the other parent's pockets or pocketbooks, the child might become confused about when it is permissible to take things from others: rules should always be spelled out clearly.

Through simple, everyday habits and routines, children can be taught respect for the rights of others, especially if their own privacy and property rights are also respected.

What you can say

What should you say if you become aware that your child has taken something in a store or from your wallet?

To the child under six, Haim Ginott has advised parents to say, "The lollipop in your left pocket has to stay in the store" when they have caught their child in the act. Don't ask the child why he stole; he doesn't really know. Address yourself to the act, not the motivation behind it. The child under six doesn't have the capacity to understand the rights of others, his own relationship to authority, or the feelings of other people. If you discover your young child taking money from your wallet, Ginott has suggested that you say,

"You took a dollar from my wallet. Give it back. You took the money. Now return it." Since the child under six isn't aware of his motivation, if you pressure him to give you a reason, he'll probably lie in addition to stealing.

What should you do if a child of six or older returns home with an article not paid for? Firmness is essential and should be maintained despite the child's attempts to justify shoplifting. Say, "It doesn't matter what the other kids did. You don't take things that don't belong to you." Remain firm, even in the face of: "But, Ma, nobody saw me," or "It's just a little thing. I didn't have the time to stand in line and wait to pay," or "The store charges too much anyway. They rip you off." In all cases the child should return the stolen item. If, however, his embarrassment is so great that he cannot bring himself to do it, you might do it for him, but then administer an appropriate punishment at home. If the stolen object has been consumed, given away, or destroyed, the child should pay for it. Explain the realistic consequences of theft — embarrassment, arrest, the possibility of a police record; appeal to immediate considerations, not high moral principles: "It makes you feel bad," or "You'll get in trouble," or "I will not allow it."

For the child above nine years, it's important also to tackle moral principles, by explaining the consequences to others. This should be done in terms that relate to the child: "If you were allowed to steal from others, they would also have the right to steal from you. What about that? Would you like it if someone took your new bike or your roller skates?"

Parental reactions such as "Don't you know that stealing is a sin?," or "After all we've done for you, is this how you repay us?," or "What will the neighbors say?" are not usually helpful, because they avoid dealing with the crucial issues — the child's feelings and the realistic consequences of the act.

An older child can understand motivation. Help your children come to understand why they stole by exploring with them alternative ways in which they might have solved the predicament that prompted them to steal: "What else could you have done?," or "Where else could you have gotten the money?," or "What are some ways that you could have told the other kids you didn't want to do it?"

D. W. Winnicott, the late British pediatrician and psychoanalyst, suggested another approach to helping children understand their motivations. In advising a mother what she might say to a son who had a compulsion to steal from stores as well as at home, he suggested that the mother wait until there was a good moment in her relationship with the boy and then ". . . tell him that you know that when he steals he is not wanting the things that he steals, but he is looking for something that he has a right to; that he is making a claim on his mother and father because he feels deprived of their love." Winnicott suggested that the mother use language she knew the boy could understand.

Sometime later Winnicott received a letter from the mother telling him that she had done as he had suggested: "I told him that what he really wanted when he stole money and food and things was his mum, and I must say I didn't really expect him to understand, but he did seem to. I asked him if he thought we didn't love him because he was so naughty sometimes, and he said right out that he didn't think we did, much. Poor little scrap! I felt so awful, I can't tell you. So I told him never, never to doubt it again and if he ever did feel doubtful, to remind me to tell him again . . ."

Parents who help their children learn to respect the law aid them in forming internal restraints — a conscience. Our adult internal restraints were originally external ones: in the course of growing up, as we identified with our parents, teachers, and other role models and learned about the consequences of our acts, we internalized society's external rules, regulations, laws, and prohibitions. Parents should recognize that young children have not yet had the time or experiences that enable them to establish their internal restraints, and a conscious effort should be made to provide the outside help that they need.

Punishment — the Big Question

Interestingly, children's prescriptions for punishment are often tougher than those of adults. Jean Piaget, in studying the development of children's ideas about punishment, has determined that the earliest concepts of justice are based on retribution, the "eye for an eye, tooth for a tooth" principle. Preschoolers believe that whoever misbehaves must be punished severely, no matter what the crime:

David, 5½: "Spank him. Don't let him watch TV. Make him sit in a corner for a whole day."

Iris, 5½: "Whip them very bad. Everybody has to learn not to steal."

Morrie, five: "Lock them in their room for a week."

It also seems natural to the young child that a misdeed should automatically bring about its own punishment. Knives hurt children who touch them when they have been told not to; bridges collapse under children who cross them when they have been forbidden to.

From about seven to eight years on, children advocate that the punishment fit the crime, such as being put to bed when one has pretended to be too sick to go to school, or in the case of stealing:

Richard, seven: "My mother would make me put it back. If I opened it already, she'd have to pay the lady for it."

Jack, seven: "If I took something away from somebody else, I'd have to give them something back to make it even."

From ten years on, children can take into account individual motives, circumstances, age, and experience. When asked how they would deal with stealing, some children responded:

Clara, ten: "I wouldn't hit my kids if they would steal because then they'd do it again for spite. So I'd tell them not to do it because it's bad. It's not right."

Felice, eleven: "They should talk to them at first. I know it hurts parents when they see that their children are out there stealing and doing all this stuff."

Tom, twelve: "If a kid stole from my store, first I would think of how it was when I was little, and I know that I would feel bad. I would think back to my childhood and try to scare him. If he came back again, I would forget about my childhood and do whatever any other store owner would do — take their name and call their parents."

Arnie, eleven: "If my kid steals, I'm the type that would sit down and talk to him, tell him it was wrong. I wouldn't act very disappointed. I wouldn't beat him, but maybe the next time I would put him on punishment for about a week because stealing's wrong."

Remember: *Stealing* means taking something that belongs to somebody else, and very young children don't understand that things may belong to their parents, to playmates, or to a store, and not to them. Thus, parents cannot expect young children, who don't as yet understand the idea of private property, to consider taking something stealing. Do teach your children the distinction between *mine* and *yours,* but recognize that until they clearly understand it, their taking things probably arises out of curiosity rather than a criminal impulse.

Keep your answers simple. Don't try to explain complexities such as the profit motive or the process of justice to a child under the age of seven. You will not be very successful.

Why can't I take the Mars Bar [ice cream, candy, sneakers]?

"There's a rule against it. It belongs to the storekeeper. We have to pay for things we get from the store."

I want to keep this book. It's my favorite book in the whole world. Why can't I have it? Susan's mother let her keep a library book.

"It belongs to the library. I know it's your favorite book and I wish you could keep it. You have to give it back so other children can check it out. You can take the books out that the other children bring back."

Some Typical Questions of Older Children
Easy ones

Everybody in my crowd shoplifts. They'd throw me out of the group if I didn't go along with them. Why can't I take something once in a while? I won't get caught.

It's important that in answering you communicate your concern. Don't remain too cool.

"Sooner or later, you'll get caught. I don't want you to get in trouble. If you hang out with kids who steal — even if you yourself don't steal — you might be the one that gets caught. Shoplifting is dangerous. The stores have mirrors and TV cameras and detectives. You can't tell who the store detectives are, because they don't wear uniforms like the police. They look like anybody who would be shopping in the store."

Harder ones

Leslie's father told the conductor he was five and he could ride free. But Leslie is really seven. The cashier gave Lynn an extra dollar change and her mother said it was all right to keep it, the cashier should be more careful. Is that stealing?

Here's a dilemma for you! Who hasn't tried to save money by telling a white lie about a child's age, by keeping a quarter returned in error? Maybe you haven't. But if you found change in a telephone coin box, would you send it to the telephone company?

What happens if your child finds out that you, as most people, take minor liberties with the rules, that you, as most people, do not always follow the exact letter of the law?

Beginning at about eight years of age, children compare two things: what you say and what you do. If they detect a clash between the two, they're more likely to model themselves on what you do than on what you say, especially if what you do brings pleasure.

Try to be as consistent as possible. If you tell your child to return a nickel that was given to her in error and yet you admit, or even boast, that you didn't declare extra income on your tax return, it creates a conflict. Older children are particularly sensitive to evidence of hypocrisy.

Why did this guy get a long jail term for a robbery when all he stole was a hundred dollars? This other guy didn't pay fifty-nine thousand dollars in taxes and when they caught him he didn't have to go to jail, he only had to pay a fine. Do you call that equality before the law?

Use your children's questions to encourage discussion about social inequities. Are you tempted to defend the status quo to your child? Or are you willing to engage in a discussion about what is and what might be, whether some laws need changing?

Growing up means losing illusions about a perfect or perfectible society. But growing up also permits children to be realistic about what action they might take to change existing inequities. Help your children decide what they might do. Teen-agers often become reformers after they discover injustices — both in the family and in society. Encourage them and help them work for causes they select.

8

Money, Work, and Unemployment

"The Dow-Jones index fell 5.6 points and trading was heavy."

"The price of gold rose again."

"The money supply will be tightened."

ALTHOUGH WE HEAR such items on newscasts, few of us understand their significance. What makes the Dow index fluctuate? Who sets the price of gold or tightens the money supply? Such questions are complex and, fortunately, far removed from children's everyday concerns. Younger children will not ask about them, and by the time teen-agers ask we can send them to the library to find the answers for all of us. Younger children's questions are more immediate, practical, and personal: Can I have more allowance? Can I have my own color TV like Toby, next door? Can we buy the car I saw on channel four? Why are you mean to me but you just got a new car [washing machine, stereo, tennis racket]? Why don't they just print more money when we need it?

Money

What do children know about it and how do they learn it?

To toddlers, money is a toy, a metal chip. They soon learn that it differs from other toys; it doesn't break and get thrown into the garbage can, you're allowed to play with pennies, not with quarters, and never with paper money. To a three-year-old, more money means more coins.

Five-year-olds can distinguish nickels and pennies by name, but not by value. They consider one coin "a little money" and many coins "a lot of moneys"; they prefer larger coins to smaller ones, many pennies to one dime. The shinier and newer the penny, the more desirable and valuable it is, and the more eagerly it is exchanged for a dirty old dime. Once children learn to pass up a new penny for an old dime, they're catching on to what money is all about.

Children learn about numbers in the course of growing up even without formal instruction. But they don't really understand numbers until long after they learn to recite them or even to repeat simple arithmetical facts: they can tell you that one plus one is two, but fully understanding it is something else again.

Several ideas are involved. First, there is the idea that the number one refers to one thing, the number two to two things, and so forth, a notion called "one-to-one correspondence." A number concept also implies this idea: five things are five things no matter where they're located — side by side, scattered all over the room, or in California. When children understand that the placement of the items is irrelevant, that the number remains the same, they've taken a major intellectual step, one that rarely occurs before the age of five or six.

Also basic to understanding money is the idea that five cents can be represented either by five individual pennies or by one nickel. When a father offered his son a nickel in exchange for five pennies, the boy refused, saying, "I feel richer this way."

With experience, children learn that the value of money lies in what you can buy with it rather than in how many coins you actually have. They also learn that once you spend your money, you don't have it anymore, so you can't spend it on something else. Children also learn from experience that you get in trouble if you just help yourself to somebody else's money.

Five-year-olds know that money is exchanged for goods, but they can't understand the meaning of the exchange itself. They see giving the money as a ritual, a custom. What the storekeeper does with the money is unclear.

These are the ideas of 5½-year-old Tracy, who was interviewed (in England) by Catholic University psychologist Hans Furth:

INTERVIEWER: What does the lady at the till do with all the money?

TRACY: She gives it to the manager of the shop, who counts it out by night and gives it to different people.

INTERVIEWER: What sort of different people?

TRACY: Well, like the mayor or somebody like that.

INTERVIEWER: That's interesting, tell me a bit more about that. Where is the mayor?

TRACY: Well, he's in London, really.

INTERVIEWER: What does he do with the money?

TRACY: He spends it on jewelry and stuff for his self.

INTERVIEWER: On jewelry?

TRACY: Yes, for his wife and his self.

INTERVIEWER: Does the money from all the shop managers go to the mayor?

TRACY: No, some goes to the Queen.

INTERVIEWER: And what does the Queen do with it?

TRACY: Well, she buys some more jewelry and some clothes for herself.

Some children think a store is like a bank. "If we need money, we go to the store and get the money." "The storekeeper has to give people money or they couldn't buy things."

What do children think banks are for? Five-year-olds think that if you have money you give it to the bank to keep. Then if you need some, the teller at the bank returns it to you. But if you have no money to put in the bank, the bank will still give you money: "If you're broke, you write a check," a five-year-old informed us confidently.

To get money from the bank, you again perform a ritual. You fill out a slip or you write a check, then you get the money. Who's allowed to write a check? Certainly not children; they're too little. You have to be twenty or thirty or eighteen, and then you're allowed to have your own checkbook.

Language adds its own confusions. People are said to "make money." One of our four-year-old informants spoke of a money-making machine, which he thought was located in the basement of his father's place of work. We use many words that depend on familiarity with basic ideas about the relationship of numbers and money; words such as *cheap, expensive, bargain* don't mean much to young children. Neither does exhorting them to "save for a rainy day"; they don't understand the idea of putting things off.

Not until six or seven do children begin to put these ideas together. Even then, although they know the value of most coins, they don't grasp the idea of making change. They know that they get change when they pay an incorrect amount, but they think you get back more change if you're nice than if you're mean. They personalize the customer's relationship to the storekeeper or cashier. By eight, they realize that they'll get whatever change is due to them, regardless of personality.

Ideas of credit, of the middleman, and of the profit motive are more abstract and intangible, and therefore develop more slowly. Profit is a particularly complex notion because it involves a number of invisible steps — buy low, sell high, pay expenses and taxes, then keep the difference, if there is any.

As children master number concepts, they're more realistic about money, but they still can't imagine large sums of money, just as it is hard for adults to visualize the size of our military budget or the gross national product.

The child as consumer

Scott Ward, associate professor of business administration at Harvard University, and two associates made a study in 1977 of how children learn to buy. Among other factors, they investigated the influence of television commercials on children's buying habits. Most children watch about thirty hours of television a week, and sixteen minutes of every hour of children's programs are used for commercials. Since in one year (1977) $100 million was grossed by the networks from children's shows alone, it is obvious that television has a powerful impact on children's ideas about money and buying.

Ward and his associates interviewed more than 600 mothers and children in Minneapolis–St. Paul and Boston. The younger the children, they found, the less attention they paid to the content of either the television program or the commercial. Five-year-olds usually recalled only a single element: ["there was a man on a horse or a lady in a car, or a pussycat eating]." With increasing age, they recalled more elements of what they had seen and related them in the proper sequence.

What were the children's reactions to television commercials? Do children believe commercials tell the truth? Ward and his associates found that about fifty percent of the kindergarten children didn't think advertising was always truthful. This percentage increased as the children got older, and by the sixth grade many children felt that commercials lie "most of the time." From about third grade on the children related specific experiences with the products that weren't satisfactory ("it didn't work right"; "it fell apart"; "it was smaller than they showed"). The sixth graders knew that products are sold to make money and that the manufacturer may make the product look better than it is in order to sell it. In spite of this skepticism, however, the children reported that they wanted many of the things advertised.

Ward and his colleagues found that children become more sophisticated consumers as they grow older. The children in the study were asked, "Suppose you wanted to buy a new television set. What would you want to know about it?" Although the older children also considered performance and price, appearance was important at all ages. Remember, when your six-year-old comes home with an attractively packaged, overpriced, flashy, unworkable toy, that talking about the relative qualities of products will have little meaning!

Parents' attitudes

Some of your own early experiences and your parents' attitudes toward money probably influence your habits and ideas about thrift, generosity, budgeting, and so on, and you in turn will transmit some of the same feelings to your children. You may wish to raise your child as you were raised, or else as you wish you had been raised. Was money freely available to you when you were a child? Were your parents unemployed? in debt? rich but frugal? poor but generous? living on public assistance? Are your present attitudes toward money tinged by your parents' worries of long ago? Despite your early experiences, whatever they were, you probably want your children to be reasonable and realistic about money, to be neither misers nor big-time spenders.

Parents often make assumptions about money that are labeled "common sense," but which are contradicted by some current research findings. Professors Helen Marshall and Lucille Magruder, of the University of Kentucky, investigated how parents' practices affect children's knowledge and use of money. Will your children necessarily adopt your attitudes? Not completely, discovered Marshall and Magruder. Although your children are undoubtedly influenced by you, they don't always adopt your attitudes toward money and other possessions, or toward anything else, for that matter. Even if money is all-important to you, it may not be to your children; money may mean little to you, but it could mean a great deal to your children.

Another "common sense" theory with which Marshall and Magruder disagree is that earning money necessarily teaches children more about its value than does receiving it as a gift or an allowance. In their study, the children who knew most about money were those who were given wide experience with it to spend and opportunities to save it. Another important finding was that the more financially knowledgeable children came from families in which the parents handled their income wisely, that is, in accordance with money-management principles. Another case of practice what you preach!

Try and figure out your own feelings about money. You may have some outmoded "common-sense" notions, such as that too much money will make your children spendthrifts, children must learn they can't have everything they want, and deprivation is the way to build character.

Helping children learn about money

Let young children manage simple transactions in order to learn that money is a medium of exchange.

Since children under five don't have a sense of time, don't expect them to appreciate the importance of saving. Delaying immediate pleasure in exchange for a long-term satisfaction is not possible for the young child.

Don't be surprised if young children are attracted by the appearance of a toy without considering its quality or ability to sustain interest.

ALLOWANCES

A businesslike approach works best. Two factors must be considered. The first is your general attitude toward the child's right to manage her own money; obviously, the child's age is a factor here. The other factor covers the practical considerations. You must decide the following questions:

What are the child's needs?

What should the allowance cover? Increase the items as the child gets older — the young child can deal with immediate pleasures, such as candy and toys, whereas the older child can plan for movies and gifts. By their late teens, most children should be managing many of their daily expenses.

When will allowance day be?

Will household chores be tied to the allowance?

What about emergencies?

Is part of the allowance earmarked for savings? If so, gear the savings to something specific and realistically attainable — a bicycle or a vacation, rather than a college education, for example. Reaching the goal and being congratulated for it help reinforce the positive consequences of saving.

Try to be cool about mistakes, which are inevitable. Don't automatically rescue a child with extra money, but offer support and advice without moralizing. Don't say, "When I was your age, I didn't have any money at all to buy things, and there you go, throwing yours away." In an emergency, you may have to give an advance.

Don't use money as punishment — don't cancel or reduce an allowance for a wrongdoing. If your children break windows, for example, find a punishment that fits the crime: let them pay for the damage out of their allowance in installments. If an allowance is withheld as punishment, children may equate love and acceptance with money, so keep praise and criticism separate from money.

A request by a child for a bigger allowance resembles an employee's asking for a raise. The adult experiences the granting of the raise as a sign from the boss of confidence, esteem, love, affection, or reward, and sometimes as a triumph. Conversely, an employer's refusal to grant a raise or a promotion may activate anger, rage, and disappointment. Try to remember that children may experience similar reactions when parents (even for good reason) refuse a request for more money, privileges, or things.

The child's request for a bigger allowance may have a hidden agenda. He may be communicating to you one of these messages:

Show me you love me, or love me more than a brother or sister.

Show me that you're willing to grant me power and independence.

Agree with me that I can manage money but I need more than I'm getting.

I want to show the other kids I have more money than they have.

Discuss family financial matters openly. Children can sense when something is wrong and the best way to ease their worry is to acknowledge the problem. Family discussions give everyone a chance to talk about their opinions and are a way of making parental values explicit. When your children ask how you arrive at decisions about allowances, a statement about the family budget makes sense: "We've budgeted x amount of money for your allowances. We've budgeted money for a vacation, for a new television set, for a car [or whatever]. Next year we may be able to give you more money." A reference to a budget is less emotional — more neutral — and therefore more acceptable to a child than a parent's assertion of power, such as "Don't question my decisions," or "I think that's enough money for you at your age," or "Don't ask me why."

SOME TYPICAL DILEMMAS

Young children spend money impulsively: An eight-year-old complains about his five-year-old brother, "We both get allowances but he spends his the minute he gets it. That's O.K. with me. But when I buy something from my savings, he starts nagging and nagging because he has no money left. I tried to explain saving to him, but it didn't work."

In such a case you might explain to your eight-year-old that age has something to do with the ability to save, that an appreciation of future need is more usual with eight-year-olds than with five-year-olds.

Sibling conflict may occur when one child works:

"My sister is eighteen and she gets a lot of credit," says an eleven-year-old. "She makes money and spends it on people. One day she bought my mother a ring and my mother said that was nice of her, five times! I can't buy her much because I don't have a job and I only get a small allowance . . ."

In this case the problem is phrased in terms of money but it really seems to be a request on the part of the child for approval from the mother.

Parents and children don't always agree on how money is best spent: "I play the violin and I hate it," states a fifth grader. "I tried to talk my father into letting me quit but he won't let me. I hate the orchestra and the conductor. I have to wake up early to get ready for orchestra. Some other kids want to quit, too, but their parents won't let them. My father is paying a lot of money on what I don't like."

Here parent and child might negotiate in order to come to some compromise, such as the child's agreeing to continue with the violin for a designated trial period. If the child continues to hate playing, she won't be much of a musician and the money might indeed be wasted.

Work

"What do you want to be when you grow up?" is a question often asked of children of all ages. To young children the question doesn't make much sense. They know something about money and something about work, but they don't connect the two ideas.

We asked a group of first graders in Rego Park, New York,

questions about their parents' work. They told us that their mothers and fathers cook and clean at home, they go to work on the train or by car, to a big building with an elevator and a water cooler, or a factory, studio, office, or school. Although they were specific and detailed about their parents' work at home, their ideas about what parents do when they work away from home were a mixture of fact and fantasy. Even when parents had taken the children to their places of work, the children remembered only what was salient to them — where the pencils were, where the coffee machine was, whether they were allowed to play with typewriters, computers, sewing machines, whatever. We questioned the same group of children on what the President did all day and how he got money to take care of his family. Six-year-old Tim thought that the President spent his time taking care of the world, seeing that nobody started a war, and talking to people on television, but that in addition he had to work to earn money, like Tim's father — perhaps he too worked in a furniture store.

How do young children think people acquire occupations? The idea is a complex one, because training for most occupations takes a certain amount of time. The process of becoming a photographer, salesperson, dentist, dressmaker goes on over a period of study and experience, and young children can't fathom processes that continue over time — such as education, pregnancy, or the process of justice. They're impatient and in their minds the preparation for an occupation is simplified. For five-year-old Kiera, all you have to do is grow up.

INTERVIEWER: How do you get to be a nurse?
KIERA: I just grow up to be a nurse.
INTERVIEWER: If you just grow, can you be a nurse?
KIERA: Yes.
INTERVIEWER: How do you think you get to be a teacher?
KIERA: You just grow up to be a teacher.

This is six-year-old Jane's view of how people become teachers:

JANE: They sign up in school.
INTERVIEWER: They tell the school they want to be teachers?
JANE: Yes, they let her be a teacher and she gives them money. She pays the principal.

Some children believe that acquiring the tools of the trade is sufficient:

INTERVIEWER: How do you get to be a policeman?
TERRY, six: You go to the store where they have the costumes and you buy one, and a whistle and a gun and a stick and a badge.
INTERVIEWER: And then you're a policeman? Do you do anything else?
TERRY: You have to be big, like twenty-one.

Once you choose an occupational role, you stick with it always:

INTERVIEWER: If you're a policeman, can you be something else, too?
TERRY: No, you can't. You're a policeman, you don't change.
INTERVIEWER: How long will you be a policeman?
TERRY: I think until you die.

Seven-year-old Brad adds preparation as a requirement:

INTERVIEWER: What do you want to be when you grow up?

Brad: Uh, play football. I want to play defense — a line-backer.

Interviewer: How do you get to be a football player?

Brad: Well, you start in Little League and then you practice and work your way up.

Even older children, who have a more realistic picture of their parents' work, still don't quite understand the complex processes involved in employment. A nine-year-old told us about his mother's selling real estate: "She gets paid three thousand five hundred dollars by the people who have the house when the new people buy it." "Why three thousand five hundred dollars?" "It's half the price of the house."

When do children become aware of differences in occupational prestige? In our culture most adults agree on the amount of prestige a given occupation has, and by the time children reach adolescence they share the adults' view. That is, they usually rank professionals and business executives on top of the scale and unskilled occupations at the bottom.

But what about younger children? How do they rank occupations? Twenty boys* in each grade in the Palo Alto public schools were asked to rank eleven jobs in order of their standing in the community. Each boy was also asked to rank his father's job and the job he himself intended to have and to give reasons for his placement of each job.

The typical first and second grader knew eight or nine of the eleven jobs on the list and could pick out the job he felt had the best standing, although he could not really rank all of them. He typically rated his expected job number one, especially if that was also his father's job. First and second graders equated what they considered dangerous jobs with high standing in the community. Policeman was most often given a number one rating. A teacher's job was also consid-

* No reason was given by researcher Barbara Gunn for the omission of girls.

ered important because a teacher "helps you learn numbers up to a hundred,.maybe three thousand," or is important "because if you're climbing up a tree and get stuck, a teacher helps you out."

By about age eight, the children were able to rank jobs on the basis of their importance to the community. A father's job was no longer prestigious just because one's father performed it. Policeman was no longer included among the number-one occupations by all children, doctor now getting many more votes. Relatively unskilled workers, such as janitors, were now ranked at the bottom of the scale. By eleven or twelve, the children increasingly used criteria other than service to the community as indicators of prestige — money, psychological rewards, education required, power. These children's rankings of prestige were essentially the same as adult rankings.

Unemployment — the Meaning of Job Loss
For the adult

Whether a job is experienced as pleasant or unpleasant, its loss usually causes pain. The loss of income and status are frightening, but even beyond that, job loss has important symbolic meanings: getting laid off or fired reminds one of being excluded, rejected, unloved. One feels inadequate, hopeless, powerless, depressed. Moreover, a parent may be angry with the boss who fired him or her, and may displace the anger onto a spouse or powerless child. With unemployment, a previously patient parent can become moody, bitter, and unpredictably explosive.

For the child

Young children comprehend neither why people go to work nor why they stop working. What they react to after a par-

ent's loss of a job is a family crisis: something dreadful has
happened, the parents are angry and unhappy. Whose fault
is it? Younger children may feel that they are the cause of
the crisis, that the present trouble is a punishment for something they've done, a reaction similar to what they experience
in other crisis situations.

Although children may know what money is and that parents go to work, they are still unsure of the link between
work and earning money, and thus the loss of a parent's job
and the ensuing belt tightening may not result in the young
child's asking immediate direct questions. We asked a five-
year-old what his parents would do if they had no more
money; he thought that they could always write a check and
give it to the people at the supermarket. To some children,
"having no money" means not seeing any around the house,
that is, it might be somewhere else.

Sooner or later, parental unemployment affects children
in several ways. At first the child may notice that his mother
or father is home more. Studs Terkel, in his book *Working*,
talks about the changes in his family life due to a job loss:
". . . I had just barely started school and all of a sudden the
man I saw only rarely for a few moments here and there was
suddenly around all the time. It was a shock to me."

When fewer toys are bought or a vacation trip is canceled,
a child may ask why things have changed. If the parent was
fired and if the loss of the job meant not only loss of income
but also loss of status and happiness, the child's questions
may plunge the unemployed parent into a terrible mood, reinforcing the child's fears that she has caused the trouble.

How can a parent explain the causes of his/her unemployment to a child? Young children lack both the necessary vocabulary and the experience to comprehend the situation;
they cannot imagine why a parent is unemployed. They can't
deal with concepts such as a personality clash with a superior,
a job without challenge or advancement, retrenchment, ex-

cessing, technological changes. Language is crucial. When a five-year-old was told that her father had been fired, she began to cry. Why was she crying? Not because she could imagine the consequences of the job loss to the family. No, to her there was a more immediate danger: she pictured the firing done with a match and thought her father had been burned.

Young children personalize employer-employee relationships, which confuses their understanding of the job loss. They are apt to see unemployment as a punishment. They may have previously envisioned a parent's boss as a powerful and benevolent person, similar perhaps to the President, or God. Now the boss has been mean to Mommy or Daddy and fired her or him. If in fact parents communicate that they feel betrayed by a superior, the child's fantasy of a conflict-free, reward-for-virtue world may undergo shocks, and doubt and anxiety may ensue.

Some Typical Children's Questions

Brett, six, whose father lost his job asked, "Are we poor now? Are we going to have money for food?"

Amy, seven, after hearing that her mother, a single parent, had lost her job, asked nothing and said nothing but began to hoard food in her room.

Since children are totally dependent on their parents, they panic easily. Reassure the child that you will always have food, that when people run out of money they can borrow some, or go on welfare, or get food stamps. Sooner or later you'll get a new job. Add that everybody in the family will probably have to give up some nonessentials, but not food.

Did you get fired because you were bad?

Although very young children don't understand the impersonal employer-employee relationship, you might begin to teach it. Clarify how employers look for employees with certain skills who are willing to work certain hours for a certain amount of money, and that sometimes arrangements don't work out, for any number of reasons.

By seven or eight years, children understand that employer-employee relationships are impersonal, that people don't get fired because they're "bad," and that they don't get new jobs because they're "good."

When will you get another job? The hidden agenda may be "Will you *ever* get another job? Are we going to be poor now?"

"I'm looking and soon I'll find something I like and can do and get enough money for."

The overall economic situation in the country is less important in answering children's questions or in making explanations than your own state of mind. Don't cite unemployment statistics; rather, describe in concrete terms what took place, why you are now out of work, the actual effects on the family budget, and what changes will have to be made. Explain the reasons for moving to a less expensive apartment or giving up music lessons, vacations, the car. It is crucial to transmit to your child that the family will adapt and weather the storm.

9

Religion

Catholic and Protestant and Jewish are different ways of voting for God.

— NINA, seven years old

WHETHER PROTESTANT, Jewish, Catholic, Moslem, atheist, or whatever, all children ask similar questions about religion at given ages. Your child's age, however, is not the only factor that will determine how you answer questions about religion. Your religious affiliation and your beliefs and their intensity will color your answers. In general, religious parents feel more comfortable than nonreligious ones when their children ask questions about faith, just as religious parents have an easier time responding to their children's questions about death. Children long to be told that life will continue after death, and the believing parent can calm a child's fears by speaking of God's will, his wish to have us by his side, his releasing us from our earthly suffering, and of a better life in the hereafter.

These questions, and all questions related to religion, create a problem for nonbelieving parents or for parents who can be described as partial believers; that is, people who are aware of a spiritual force and feel the need to transmit their cultural heritage but are unwilling to participate in formal rituals. Some parents have an additional problem in that they may not share a religion or have the same attitude about their children's religious upbringing.

What does religion mean to children at different stages of their lives?

As we have noted in other chapters, the younger children are, the more they pay attention to the concrete and the obvious. Differences in skin color are easy to spot; differences in people's beliefs are tougher to identify. Moreover, young children don't have the vocabulary you need to talk about religion. Education professors George Kaluger and Clifford Kolson studied the religious speaking vocabulary of 500 kindergarten children in Pittsburgh, Portland, Oregon, and Washington, D.C., public schools. They found that the children rarely used religious words. Out of almost a million words recorded during play activities, only 34 religious ones were employed, and these less than 1,500 times. As might be expected, the more tangible words — those related to specific events or activities — headed the list: *Christmas, Christmas tree, church, prayer, angel,* and *God.*

The children were shown pictures of the Star of David and the Easter Bunny among other images of religious holidays. Although they knew what the pictures meant, they didn't talk about them during play. Young children understand more words than they use, but Kaluger and Kolson suggest that the thinking and questioning of kindergarten children about religion in particular — a largely abstract subject — is limited by their vocabulary.

When children do talk about religion, we can't be certain that the meanings they attach to the words are correct. Children can glibly recite prayers, but often they don't understand the words. One five-year-old said God's name was Harold, like her cousin's. How did she know? It said so in the prayer she learned, ". . . Harold be thy name." Another five-year-old said she prayed to Art. Art who? "Art in heaven."

The Concept of Religious Denomination

Very young children frequently confuse the religious label with national, ethnic, racial, or other labels. Their category system isn't always the same as ours: said 4½-year-old Emily, "Mommy, are we Jewish or vegetarians?" A five-year-old answered the question "Are you Lutheran *and* American?" with "I'm a Lutheran when I'm awake. When I sleep, I'm American."

The psychologist David Elkind investigated children's ideas about their denominations, speaking to hundreds of Protestant, Catholic, and Jewish children between the ages of four and twelve. No matter what the religion, Elkind found similar ideas at similar ages. For example, four- to six-year-olds have fuzzy notions about their religious affiliation and consider it a name. Five-and-a-half-year-old Pat was asked whether her family was Protestant. "Our name is Blackmur," she replied. Elkind asked again if she was Protestant. "No" (wistfully), "just plain Blackmur."

When Elkind asked how one becomes Jewish, or Catholic, or Protestant, the four- to six-year-olds thought they had always been what they were, or that their parents or God had decided on what they were to be.

The seven- to nine-year-olds in Elkind's study were clearer about denominations but they still thought of a denomination as a specific activity rather than a belief. You go to mass if you're Catholic, to temple or Hebrew school if you're Jewish. You can't be both Catholic and Protestant, because "you can't go to two churches." But you can be both American and Catholic at the same time, because "you can live in America and go to church."

How can you tell if a person is a Catholic? The seven- to nine-year-olds thought you could tell if you saw the person go into a Catholic church. They thought you were Jewish if you were born into a Jewish family.

Elkind found ten- to twelve-year-olds' thinking about religion to be more abstract than younger children's. These older children no longer defined a denomination by mentioning names ("Blackmur") or observable activities, but rather by speaking about such nonobservable qualities as belief and understanding. "A Jew is a person who believes in one God and doesn't in the New Testament." "A Catholic believes in the truths of the Roman Catholic Church." Could someone be both American and Protestant? "Yes, one is a nationality and one is a religion. They're two different things."

How can you tell if someone is Catholic? Ten- to twelve-year-olds said: "If they go to mass," or "If they cross themselves before a Catholic church," or "If they say bad words, they're not Catholics," or "You can't tell, you have to ask them." The ten- to twelve-year-olds were familiar with initiation practices and ritual: "Until you're bar mitzvahed you're not a real Jew."

The word *Protestant*, which covers nearly three hundred different groups, confuses children. The children Elkind interviewed considered themselves Lutherans, Congregationalists, Episcopalians, and so on, rather than Protestants. The word *Jewish* is also confusing in that it covers several categories; in addition to referring to a denomination, *Jewish* is a label for an ethnic group — one may belong to the ethnic group without sharing the religious beliefs, and one may adopt the religious beliefs without being ethnically Jewish. Moreover, *Jewish* is also a national or political label, as in "the Jewish state." In view of such complexities it is a wonder that children do eventually disentangle the labels and learn who belongs and who does not belong to each group — usually at about eleven or twelve years.

Concepts of God

Young children view God as a specific person, a type of father, capable of protecting them but living away from the family, somewhere in the sky, on a cloud. One five-year-old drew us a picture of God as Superman. Another explained that God was greater than Superman, Batman, and the Lone Ranger put together. Before the age of six, children barely distinguish God from good-natured giants or other kind-hearted supernatural folk. They consider God responsible for natural events: he blows air to make wind, he throws lightning bolts and bumps the clouds together to make thunder.

Five-year-old Miranda discussed her dead dog: "I'm glad he has a new family with God. Lots of angels up there. My dog is an angel. The pound let her go up to God and now she's an angel. Aunt Myrtle died. She's up in heaven with my dog, so she could watch, and God watches, too."

Children acquire their first ideas of God from many sources in addition to their parents — from movies, stories, television, other children, and places of worship. Nonbelieving parents are surprised (even embarrassed!) about how much their children learn in spite of the fact that no one in the family has mentioned God. Regardless of their source, young children's ideas about God refer to a concrete person rather than to an abstract idea. And since they view their parents as all-powerful, all-knowing, and totally dependable, they attribute these same qualities to God.

Young children will accept God on the parents' say-so, and it is during the early years that the picture of a loving or punitive God evolves. If parents are gentle, loving people, they'll probably depict God in the same way; if they're inclined to be more stern, they'll probably stress the judge and punisher variety of God. Children may ask questions during these years, but the questions are more likely to be information-seeking than argumentative or skeptical.

Older children abandon their earlier, more literal ideas about God. Capable of abstract thinking, they begin to formulate more personal and individualistic ideas. While some accept ideas of God current in their families, others search for ideal images, utopian societies and perfect families. For the latter, God as the embodiment of the good offers hope. Others abandon religion altogether.

Prayer

Elkind and his associates also investigated children's ideas of prayer. They interviewed 160 children from all the major religious groups on whether they prayed, where they thought prayers come from, how they felt when they prayed, and other questions.

Between the ages of five and seven, these children had only vague notions of prayer. Although they were dimly aware that prayers are somehow linked with the word *God* and with certain sayings, the meaning of prayer was not understood. It is something you do, but they didn't know why. For them, prayer is a ritual to be observed before going to bed, in church or synagogue, before or after eating. At these ages children pray obediently, without much feeling.

One of Elkind's informants, almost six years old, told him that "a prayer is about God, rabbits, dogs and fairies and deer, and Santa Claus and turkeys and pheasants, and Jesus and Mary and Mary's little baby." Another child, 5½, said, "A prayer is God bless people who want to say God bless. Now I lay me down to sleep . . ."

Although the meaning of prayer eluded these children, some prayers seem to add to children's fears, as suggested by a "Dear Abby" letter: "While saying a goodnight prayer with my four-year-old grandchild, when we came to the part 'If I should die before I wake' she stopped abruptly, and with a very frightened expression on her little face she asked, 'Nana, do you think I *will* die before I wake?' "

In the book *Children's Letters to God,* by E. Marshall and S. Hample, children write: "Dear God, I saw Saint Patrick

Church last week when we went to New York. You live in a nice house." "Dear God, Church is all right, but you could sure use better music. I hope this does not hurt your feelings." "Dear God, could you write more stories? We already read all the ones you have and begin again."

For the seven- to nine-year-olds in Elkind's study, the idea of prayer had clearly changed. They still thought of prayer as an activity but one that is different from others. It is more like a request that God could grant. They knew now that not everyone prays. Why not? Some people don't pray because "They forget," or "They're too sleepy," or "They don't want anything." These children also indicated that God has a limited capacity to grant their requests, that not everyone can be served completely and at once.

Between the ages of ten and twelve, prayer is often a private conversation with God, involving things not talked about with other people. A ten-year-old told Elkind that "Prayer is a way to communicate with God . . . to ask him forgiveness, to ask him if something would go right when it's going wrong." Prayers now have an ethical aspect, and they become more personal; these children use fewer ready-made prayers. They often pray for the good of the family or the community — one of their most frequent requests is for everyone in their family to remain healthy and not die. At these ages there is also a concern for humanity, and God is often asked to help maintain peace, clean up polluted air, stop crime, and so forth. What these children pray for has become more specific than in earlier years but is not necessarily a favor for themselves.

As the meaning and content of children's prayers change with age, so do their feelings while praying. Older children engage in prayer less perfunctorily and more spontaneously than younger children, in response to particular feelings — when they are worried, lonely, troubled — although they will also continue to pray at fixed times, as they did when they were younger.

Questionings and Crises

After the age of six or thereabouts, children begin to distinguish fairy-tale characters or Superman from religious figures, and perceive religion more realistically as an institution, as a system to adapt to. They slowly separate religious labels from national, ethnic, and other labels. When they draw pictures on religious themes they frequently use religious symbols or Biblical motifs. One seven-year-old drew a picture of God wearing a blanket and sandals and traveling on a donkey.

A crisis in children's thinking about religion, as in their thinking about the world in general, begins at about the age of six and continues for many years to come. Children discover "the human condition," that is, they come to the realization that their own and their parents' power is limited, that they, as all living organisms, must eventually die, that evil is permitted to exist, and that virtue is not always rewarded. The emotionally overwhelming experience of the discovery of the universality of death, together with the disillusionment in parental power, leads some children to become more dependent on God as a source of power and protection. With other children the disillusionment may extend even to God.

Whereas questions before this time usually refer to meanings of a word ("What is *heaven?*") or the charting of the heavenly landscape ("Where do the angels sleep?"), questions now begin to be skeptical: "If God created everybody, who created him?" "How can God see and listen to everybody at the same time?" "How could he make the world in only six days?" "How can Joseph and God both be Jesus' father?"

They now begin to note inconsistencies between belief and reality, and to question the efficacy of prayer: "Dear God, If you know so much, how come you never made the river big enough for all the water and our house got flooded and now we got to move?" "Dear God, I got left back. Thanks a lot!" Some children are still reluctant to be openly skeptical: "Dear Mr. God, How do you feel about people who don't believe in you? Somebody else wants to know." "Are you real? Some people don't believe in it. If you are, you better do something quick."

Beginning as early as six years in some cases, the ethical aspects of religion become important and questions about God frequently include the theme of good and evil. Why would God let people get sick, starve, fight in wars? Why don't we all go to heaven if he can forgive sins? Why did God let his son die? Why did God make cockroaches? or poisonous spiders? or mean people?

Children from seven to nine are strongly influenced by their peers. They start to compare their families with others in terms of religious beliefs and membership in churches or synagogues. They may question parental authority in that they have discovered that parents, too, are accountable to higher authorities, to the law and to God.

Preadolescents and adolescents, with their typically intense feelings, yearn to form personal relationships and this can affect their religious behavior. Poised between childhood and adulthood, they often turn outside the family for a different kind of security — to God directly, to a member of the clergy, to a religious youth group. In some cases, a rebellious adolescent may reject the parents' religion.

Guidelines for Parents

Answer your own questions first. Although it's important to know that you should gear your answers to your child's intellectual capacities at a given age, the content of your answers will depend on your personal religious ideas. If you are a believer and feel strongly about raising your children to be believers, you'll know what information and what attitudes you wish to transmit to them. If you're a believer but uncertain about particular beliefs or customs, you can always consult a member of the clergy.

Some people, however, have special predicaments. "I let my husband take over the religion department, because I don't believe in anything," said one mother. "We never discuss religion. It only starts a fight," said a father in a mixed marriage. There are mixed marriages of various types: a union between people of different faiths, both believers; between a believer and a nonbeliever; or variations on the above. If the parents can agree to raise their children in a particular religion, there is little problem. Similarly, there is little problem if the parents agree not to raise their children in any faith. But parents with doubts or differing beliefs have more difficulty in dealing with their children's questions and should try to reach some meeting of the minds between themselves before addressing their children's inquiries.

Whether you're religious or not, discuss ethical and spiritual ideas with your children, but do it at a time when a family or social situation warrants it. When a child misbehaves, avoid talking about the wrath of God or the torments of hell, which can terrify children. Moreover, don't use God to make your children feel guilty. Deal with the issue at hand and don't involve God. It is usually more helpful to discuss issues of belief in a positive context rather than in a punitive one. Every child misbehaves at some time — misbehavior and disobedience are part of becoming independent. Children who are told that God is always watching, that no action slips by him, are bound to become burdened with guilt.

Don't wait indefinitely for questions. Since an important part of our cultural heritage consists of religious ideas, call them to your children's attention, even if you're a nonbeliever. This is particularly important because public schools are not permitted to discuss religion, and television, comic books, or movies may distort it. The study of the Bible as literature, as an important collection of stories, is rewarding and enriching. Once you begin telling some of the Bible stories, the children will start to ask questions about the ethical aspects of religion, how we relate to one another, what our obligations are to others, the nature, purpose, and meaning of life.

Regardless of your personal beliefs, let the children know that you take their questions and discussions seriously, a factor essential to their intellectual progress and emotional well-being.

Examine your attitudes: Is it important to you that your children share your religious, or antireligious, views? Will you permit them to question your beliefs and come to conclusions that may differ from yours? Or do you feel they have to adopt your beliefs?

Children's Questions

Questions about religion seem to fall into certain categories. We'll list the categories and give examples of the kinds of questions that fall into each.

Questions about God, heaven, and the Bible

If you don't know the answer to a factual question, look it up in the Bible or a reference book. If you are religious, use the Bible as a source of religious ideas; if you're not, use it as a book of history written in ancient times, as well as a collection of ancient myths.

Children who hear the word *God* in their homes start to ask questions at an early age. Since this is a spiritual subject, you have to make your own decision about what to say. Some typical questions are:

Where does God live? Can I see God? Does God like me? Does God have a mommy? Did God make light to see what he was doing? If God is everywhere, did I squeeze him out of the kitchen? Is God married to Mother Nature?

Simple answers are appropriate: "No, you can't see God."
"God doesn't have a body. God is a spirit, like the wind."
"You can't see God, you just know he's there." And so on.
Exactly what you say to younger children is probably un-
important. Their understanding is limited, although their
imagination is not. You might encourage them to come up
with their own fantasies and then ask them exactly what
they would like to know from you. Be available when they
do ask and consult with them should they become aware of
a particular inconsistency or contradiction and want information. Help your children get books and find words in the
dictionary, and let them ask experts. It's unlikely that they
will become aware of inconsistencies until they are old
enough to deal with at least two ideas simultaneously and
realize that one contradicts the other, which usually happens
after the age of six.

Most religious educators have emphasized that parents
should try to help their children understand the abstract idea
of God instead of helping them picture the details of life in
heaven. Allow children to construct their own version of
heaven, which will satisfy them for the time being. You
really don't know the answers to specific questions. Say something about the mysterious, unknown, and incomprehensible
events that occur in the realm of religion, as well as the
limited understanding of human beings. Benjamin Spock,
the noted pediatrician, suggests that parents answer questions
about God and the Bible and heaven along the following
lines:

> The Bible is a book that was written thousands of years
> ago. It tells how God made the whole world in the begin-
> ning. It says He made the sun and the moon and the
> stars, and the mountains and the oceans. It says He made
> all the animals and birds and fishes, and finally people.
> Lots of people go to synagogue or church to sing songs
> to God, to thank Him for all the good things they have,
> like delicious food and a nice house and warm clothes.

They also ask God to help them be good. The Bible says
God lives in heaven, but we don't know where that is.
Some say it's in the sky. People can't really see God. But
they feel He's there just the same, not as a body, but as a
spirit.

For the older child, call attention to the fact that different
people have explained things in different ways. This applies
particularly to those parents who wish to stress the comparative approach, as opposed to those whose faith in a traditional
God is very strong and to whom it is important that their
children share it.

Questions about religious holidays

*Why doesn't Brian have a Christmas tree? If Joey is Jewish,
how come he has a Christmas tree? Is Chanukah better than
Christmas?*
In general, questions about holiday traditions should be
answered by telling the child that each religious denomination has its own holidays. Many of the holidays have less religious significance now than they used to and are celebrated
by many people because of the beauty and color of the
customs.

Questions about religious membership and customs

If I go to church with Amy on Easter, will I still be Jewish?
Stress that most houses of worship welcome people of all
faiths and that merely attending a service does not change
one's religion, which is a matter of belief.
*How come everybody on the block goes to church and we
don't?*
Children between the ages of six and ten are the ones most
concerned about belonging to a group and doing what others

do. Point out to them that even if the family doesn't attend services regularly, they do have a system of beliefs — you might list them. Children should also be told that, contrary to their observation about their block, there are many other families who don't attend formal services.

Why do those men wear little hats?
"Religious Jews wear a skullcap, called a yarmulke. They are required to wear one in the synagogue, school, and at mealtimes when blessings have to be offered, but nobody knows how the custom started. Some people wear yarmulkes to show that they're Jewish."
I saw the Pope on television and he wore one. Is the Pope Jewish?
"The Pope wears a cap, too, which is also worn by other high church officials, such as bishops and cardinals. But the Pope isn't Jewish. He is the leader of all the Catholics."

Theological questions, questions of dogma, skeptical questions

These questions usually don't occur before the age of six. The direct question *Do you believe in God?* should be given as honest an answer as you can formulate. Some responses that parents have found helpful include:
"We do, but we don't know just what God is like."
"We don't but lots of other people do."
"We don't, but when you're older you may decide to believe in God."
"We do. We believe that God takes care of us."
Questions in this category should result in discussions rather than being dealt with quickly. Issues such as the creation of the world in six days versus the theory of evolution, the reasons for the ten plagues, miracles, or why God permits the devil to exist may be discussed from many points of view.

A comparative approach works well here, too. What does the Bible say? What are the various interpretations of the Biblical account of the creation? For example, a less literal interpretation of the creation views each of the six days as representing billions of years, which is an effort to unite the creation myth with an account of the earth's origin according to science.

Questions about ethical issues

These are the issues usually raised by older children, about our obligations to other people and to God, the quality of our relationships to close friends, the difference between good and evil, the purpose and meaning of life.

Let's use as an example the concept of sin. To the young child who hears the word *sin* and asks about it, a believing parent might say, "It means doing something wrong," or "It's something done against the Ten Commandments," or "It's something bad a person did or thought and has to confess," or "God watches us and he knows that a lot of people do bad things, such as cheat or steal or hurt other people. We must be careful not to do these bad things, because some day we will have to pay for our sins." The definition will vary according to your religion. Keep in mind the limitations of the child's vocabulary and thought processes. One six-year-old thought a cardinal sin referred to a wrongdoing by a bird.

With the older child, explore the fact that sin has different definitions. Among Christians, exactly what constitutes a sin is defined in different ways by Roman Catholics, Greek Orthodox Catholics, and the various Protestant groups. Moreover, the concept of sin is constantly being changed and redefined. For example, not too long ago Catholics were not allowed to eat meat on Fridays, which they are now permitted to do.

The older child will be able to understand such theological distinctions as the Catholic view of two types of sin. You might say, "A sin, which is a grievance against God, is either a mortal or a venial sin. The difference between them is in the intention. If the wrongdoing was planned, if the sinner had time to reflect on her action but chose to commit the sin anyway, it is a mortal sin. If, however, the wrongdoing occurred impulsively, without premeditation, or if it is a less grievous offense, it is considered a venial sin. But action is really unnecessary, since intention alone is sufficient to be a sin: even a thought may be a sin."

An older Jewish child might be told that sin is "anything that is the opposite of good, caused by either omission or commission. Judaism holds that people are capable of good as well as evil, and a person who has sinned can always repent and start anew. The traditional defenses against a sinful way of life are prayer, Torah study, good deeds, being in the company of wise and saintly people, and, most of all, will power."

Most religions address themselves to ethical issues and Judaism and Christianity in particular consider our relations with others of primary importance. Tell your child the story about the wise man Hillel, who lived about two thousand years ago, who was asked by a pagan to tell him all about Judaism while he, Hillel, stood on one foot. Hillel responded: "That which is hurtful to you do not do to your neighbor. Everything else is commentary. Now go and study." Christ also considered the commandment "Thou shalt love thy neighbor as thyself" as one of the most important. A Tibetan Buddhist saying agrees: "Whatever is not pleasing to yourself, do not do that unto others."

10

Prejudice

PREJUDICE, according to one dictionary definition, is a judgment or opinion formed before the facts are known, literally, a pre-judgment. There are many ramifications of this meaning — intolerance; hatred of other races, creeds, regions, occupations; unreasonable bias; and so on.

Since the 1975 Education of All Handicapped Children Act, it has become illegal to discriminate against the handicapped, as well as against blacks, women, the aged, and other minorities. All handicapped children between the ages of three and eighteen must now be "mainstreamed" into the "least restrictive educational environment." This means that children with serious disabilities will become increasingly visible in schools. And as a result of their visibility, children will ask more questions about the deaf, the blind, the retarded, and other handicapped people. It is important that children be taught not to discriminate against these people.

With most topics, you can wait until your children discover the world's complexities and ask about them. With prejudice it's different. Here, too, there is a world to be discovered, but it's an ugly world. Taking early action will help your child recognize the ugliness. An early start is important because the longer children believe in an idea based on prejudice, the more likely it is to become ingrained.

How do children become prejudiced? Let's start at the beginning, with the child's ability to make distinctions. One of the first distinctions infants make is that between familiar and unfamiliar people. Infants aren't fearful at birth but they become anxious and suspicious of strangers before they're a year old. Their fearfulness is evidence that their minds are maturing and that they're beginning to distinguish people. When "stranger anxiety" appears, between five and ten months of age, babies don't want unfamiliar people to approach them or pick them up anymore. They frown, avert their eyes, cry, and try to withdraw. Watch the grandparent who hasn't seen her grandchild for a few months; she holds out her hands to pick up the baby, who seems wary at first, then holds on to his mother or father and screams.

After children learn to distinguish the familiar from the strange, they learn a second distinction — gender. Most three-year-olds know their own sex and seem to be able to classify other people by gender. Because they speak glibly about who is a boy and who is a girl, they sound as if they know more than they actually do. Many children, for instance, believe that they will not necessarily remain a boy or a girl forever. On the one hand, preschoolers believe that everything is and will remain as they first knew it. On the other hand, they believe that magic can change both gender and species: boys into girls, girls into boys, frogs into princes, princes into frogs.

Just as preschoolers are uncertain about the permanence of gender or species, they are uncertain about race. Will they always be white or black? Sociologist Judith Porter, of Bryn Mawr College, interviewed nursery-school and kindergarten children in Boston. This is how some of the white children told her black children got their color: "He got dirt on his face and his mama didn't wash him." "Little boys when they get dirty get into a colored boy and when they get clean, they get into a white boy." David, the white four-year-old son of one of our friends, was astonished, when summer came and children took off their shirts, that his black friend's body was as black as his face.

Preschoolers seem to pick up prejudices even before they can correctly identify those against whom the bias is directed. They first identify their own group, but don't know clearly who belongs and who does not. When they do become aware of other groups, they feel strongly that their own group is the best. They're automatically against other groups, even though they're unsure of what another group stands for. They consider their own country the best in the world before they even know what a country is.

Judith Porter suggests that even preschoolers are aware of the conflict called "the American dilemma," a conflict set up by the fact that we think our own group is best and, at the same time, believe in equality for all. Guilty about our preference for our own group, as well as our negative feelings toward others, we're reluctant to state them openly.

One five-year-old rejected brown dolls offered by Porter, saying, "I have a reason [for the rejection] but I can't tell you." Later the child confided, "I'll tell you why I really didn't choose any of the colored children. I don't like colored children." Discovering that expressing negative attitudes is frowned on, and feeling the uncomfortable results, seems to be part of learning prejudice in modern America.

When we compare the prejudices of younger with those of older children, we find obvious differences:

Younger children respond to what is directly observable — people's faces and bodies, how they walk and speak. Older children know about things not directly observable — personality traits, relationships, political or religious beliefs.

Growing older means that children can think in more complicated ways. They let go of some of their simple ideas. Eventually they learn that most generalizations are false, that few statements about a group will be true for all group members.

Does that mean that all people give up their prejudices as they grow older? Some obviously do, yet others become more biased as they grow older. Age is important in determining how we think, but there are other factors, too. One is education — the more education, the fewer prejudices people seem to have, or at least people are better able to be aware of and examine their prejudices. Although there are, of course, exceptions to this generalization, education offers the most hope for combating prejudice.

Let's be more specific by taking a look at children's ideas about the handicapped. How do children perceive other people in the course of growing up? Children's earliest expectations are that all people are pretty much alike in how they look, dress, move, and speak. When they do notice that some people deviate — when they see a disfigured face or missing limb, or hear unusual speech — they are frightened and try to find reasons for this "violation of expectation." As always when children meet with a new experience, they explain the new on the basis of the old and familiar. To a young child, a disabled person might resemble a broken toy; indeed, many children ask whether the "broken" person could not get "fixed." What frightens them is that if something happened to that person, it could also happen to them. But that's not all. Some children fear that the handicap is like an illness and they could catch it — as though there were handicap "germs." Some children try to explain the handicap as a punishment for being bad; since many children get spanked for misbehaving, this explanation isn't so far-fetched.

Children's fantasies about handicapped people's being punished are similar to their fantasies about their own operations. Joyce Robertson, a British child analyst, kept a diary of the reactions of her four-year-old daughter, Jean, to a tonsillectomy. She told Jean about the operation one week in advance, and from then on Jean asked her mother many questions, mostly about her fear of punishment and assault: "Jean saw a picture of a man, a prisoner being led between two policemen; and for the next twenty minutes she questioned me persistently about 'naughty' men. 'Do children go away when they are very naughty?' At lunch she talked again about knives and forks being sharp. 'They could poke our throats,' she said." Jean seemed to feel that her tonsillectomy was a punishment.

Many children, and adults as well, are anxious when they first meet a handicapped person. The handicap affects them so strongly that they will pay little attention to any other trait of the person besides the handicap. Concerned that the handicapped person will notice their discomfort, both children and adults will try to hide it. Adults often become self-conscious and formal in this situation, avoiding words related to the particular handicap. But not children. They cover their anxiety differently. Their fear of the handicapped often leads them to cruelty — they refuse to play with handicapped children and imitate and tease them. There are certainly enough names to taunt them with; just think of all the words we have for the mentally retarded, emotionally disturbed, or crippled!

Listen to Us: The Children's Express Report, consists entirely of the words of children, mostly 13 and under, who were interviewed by a group of teen-agers. In one such round-table discussion, handicapped children spoke freely of their plight.

Jeffrey, eleven: "Sometimes they tease me. They say 'Four eyes, four eyes, you blind, that's why you don't get nowhere. How you gonna be a fireman, blindbat, blindbat?"

Hugo, thirteen: "When somebody calls me crippled, I start showing off — do wheelies in my wheelchair, I curse at him . . ."

Jimmy, ten: "Sometimes people look at me strange and ask me how come one of my eyes is closed and how come I'm blind; I think that's being nosy and I don't like that. Some people play with me and some other people try to gyp me — like when we get candy, they give me the wrong kind. Or when we play Monopoly, they don't give me the right amount of money."

Similar to their ideas about the handicapped, children's ideas about the elderly undergo a change with increasing age.

Young children's ideas of time limit their understanding of growing old. Only gradually do they comprehend what is meant by such words as *age* and *time*. A seven-year-old once asked one of us whether we had seen Christopher Columbus land. Neither the future nor the past makes much sense to young children; they live in the present only.

Before they learn to tell time, many children orient themselves by mealtimes: "Can I stay outside for a long long time, like until dinner?" Or by names: "What name will I have when I'm grown up?" asked 3½-year-old Russell. Or time is confused with places in space. Six-year-old Jane looked up at the sky and said, pointing with her finger, "That's where the day comes out, and there, further up, is the night, and right up at the top is Christmas." Many children believe that the calendar "makes" time, that tearing off calendar pages or crossing out days actually brings about an advance in time.

Most young children confuse age with size. We asked Russell, "Is your mother older than you?" Russell said, "No, my daddy is bigger." We asked him who was the oldest person in the family, and he said, "My daddy." "How do you know your daddy is the oldest?" Russell: "Because he could pick me up."

To 3½-year-old Russell, and to children several years older than he, age is not continuous — people are either little or big, which to the child equals young or old. As children grow older, they add other categories: a baby, a big child, a mommy or daddy. Russell's five-year-old brother, Dougie, placed his sixteen-year-old baby sitter into a new category — "almost man."

For children under six years, only size determines a person's age, and the taller person is always believed to be the older one. Only slowly do they begin to take other traits into account. "My dog is older than me, but I'm bigger than her. I'm bigger than Lisa in the second grade, but she's older," said seven-year-old Billy.

Children place grandparents in the same class with other "big" people and don't understand at first that grandparents must be older than their parents. Nor do they know that the relationship between grandparents and parents equals that between parents and children. According to one five-year-old, "A grandmother is an extra person in the family." Like a spare tire. "My family is very close," confided six-year-old Debbie. "My grandmother is also my mother's mother."

Richard Jantz and Carole Seefeldt, of the University of Maryland, questioned three- to eleven-year-olds about their ideas and feelings about old age, as well as about getting old themselves. They interviewed 180 children, 20 at each age level, from all walks of life and from cities, small towns, and farms. Eighty-eight percent of the children knew of elderly persons within the family, but only 22 percent said they knew such persons outside of the family.

When the children were asked how they thought they'd feel when they got old, most said they expected to feel sad, terrible, mean. "My face will feel crinkled and I won't have the fun I had when I was little," one child said. Others spoke about death: "I don't want to get old," or "My eyes will feel blurry because I'll be dying soon," and so on. When the children spoke about their feelings for the elderly, their comments were usually positive, but when they described the behavior or appearance of the elderly, they commented negatively.

Most children's contact with older people usually begins with grandparents, who are frequently only middle-aged and still active (in fact, if a parent and child are sufficiently ambitious, the parent can be a grandparent by the middle thirties) .

Although some grandparents maintain their distance and show up only on birthdays or holidays, many of them are in close contact with their grandchildren, as baby sitters or household helpers. And grandparents sometimes become their grandchildren's best friends. Hardly surprising, observed a humorist: they share a common enemy!

How prejudices are learned is an issue that obviously can't be covered in one chapter. We're merely calling attention to some of the highlights, both in the development of children's ideas and in the messages conveyed by parents, books, TV, toys, and so on.

First, the parent's role in teaching prejudice: "My son seems to dislike the same kind of people I dislike," a mother told us. "Maybe it runs in the family." Prejudice doesn't have to be spelled out in order to be taught to the child. Even words are unnecessary. Minimal signs are sufficient, and you may not be aware that anything has been transmitted. The writer Lillian Smith described the process: "We were given no formal instructions in these difficult matters, but we learned our lessons well . . . we learned far more from acts than from words, more from a raised eyebrow, a joke, a shocked voice, a withdrawing movement of the body, a long silence, than from long sentences."

However, influential though parents are, there are other forces that can determine whether or not a child will become prejudiced. Researchers have found that prejudiced parents don't automatically produce prejudiced children. Good. But wait: unprejudiced parents are unfortunately not guaranteed to have unprejudiced children. Before children go to school they have often picked up nursery rhymes derogatory toward certain groups:

There was an old woman, her name it was Peg,
Her head was of wood and she wore a cork leg.
The neighbors all pitched her into the water.
The leg was drowned first, and her head followed after.

Catch a nigger by the toe.
Eeny, meeny, miny, mo,
If he hollers let him go.
Eeny, meeny, miny, mo.

And once children can be read to or can read themselves, they are bombarded with negative views about many groups.

In a study of the stereotyping of people in children's literature, Phyllis Barnum, at the University of Chicago, picked 100 books at random from all children's books published between 1950 and 1974; all were written for ages from preschool to third grade. Grandparents barely showed up in these books. When they did appear they were almost always with children, never with other adults: in more than 2,500 illustrations, old people spoke with other adults only 18 times. The elderly usually sat in their rockers and were pictured as more sickly, more passive, and less competent than — and sometimes senile and never as self-reliant as — other adults. If they worked at all, they had jobs not requiring advanced education: they were janitors, servants, storekeepers. Their behavior was always pleasant and lacked a realistic range of emotions.

In reading textbooks, other researchers found girls usually shown as needing help and protection, lacking competence, and being timid and dependent. In contrast, boys were shown to be leaders, independent, curious, assertive, brave, and clear thinkers. Will said: "I will sit in front and steer the sled, Joan. You sit in the back, so that you can hold on to me!"

Until recently, blacks were practically invisible in children's books. A 1963 review of fifteen popular children's readers concluded: "... life in the United States is in a general way easy and comfortable ... People (all white, mostly blond and 'North European' in origin) are almost invariably kind and generous ... There are other kinds of people in the world, but they live in far off countries or in days gone by; they evidently have no place on the American scene."

Although many stereotypes linger on subtly, there have been changes. In regard to the elderly, there are now stories that even describe the death of a grandparent and the child's reaction to it. In the process of destroying stereotypes, some writers have gone overboard. *Kevin's Grandma* is a story about a grandmother Kevin invents to compete with a friend's grandmother who does interesting things. In Kevin's fantasy, Grandma denies the changes that come with old age: she goes skydiving, drives and fixes her own motorcycle, climbs mountains, does yoga, eats health food, teaches karate, tames lions, and makes peanut-butter soup.

Not only are there now children's stories that deal with people of all minorities — the elderly, women, blacks, Hispanics — but there are new textbooks as well.

Television has made less of an effort, especially with old people; the elderly are practically invisible on TV. There are a few commercials about older people's problems — iron deficiencies, loose dental plates, constipation, hemorrhoids — but middle-aged performers sell the products. Serial or prime-time shows don't use older persons as main characters. The idea that one can lead a productive life despite old age is barely conveyed to children and young adults.

In addition to nursery rhymes, books, and TV, movies, comic books, and toys shape children's ideas. Even simple toys such as dolls impart a strong message. We can now buy black dolls, but we still have no handicapped dolls. There are some grandparents dolls, but they come in sets of two, as if the elderly didn't divorce or lose a mate! The limited types of dolls available may lead children to overlook important realities: that minorities exist, that people get old, that one may become ill or handicapped. This narrow view of the world may restrict children's fantasy play: they might not be able to imagine themselves in roles other than their own — young, healthy, and pretty.

Most parents and teachers frown on children's reading of

comics for their lack of literary value. George Orwell, author of *Nineteen Eighty-four,* pointed to an even more serious objection: comics also transmit stereotyped attitudes and an outdated view of society.

Old age barely is mentioned in comic books. When it is, the elderly are pictured as insignificant, weak, playing minor roles. *Black Panther* has a muscular white-haired, white-bearded aide clad in a toga saying, "Allow N' Gassi [the aide's name] to share this problem, T-Challa. After all, I am your personal aide." T-Challa: "I wouldn't add this burden to those you already bear, old man." In three more frames N' Gassi remains in his subordinate role and never gets to bear the new burden.

How About Your Prejudices?

All of us have some prejudices and we should be aware of them. But there is a big difference between harboring a prejudice against a given group — one of the many irrational ideas all of us are stuck with — and actively attempting to deprive a group of its rights, or even subtly discriminating against its members. Examine your feelings about Jews or Christians, whites or blacks, rich people or poor people, the elderly, the blind, the deaf, the spastic, the retarded, the emotionally disturbed, and others from an endless list. You yourself are probably a member of some minority group. Become aware of the images of others that you transmit to your children and ask yourself if they are what you want to convey.

General Guidelines

1. Determine what your children actually want to know. Questions about how old Grandma is, why that child sits in

a wheelchair, whether blacks can get sunburned are not necessarily motivated by prejudice. Don't panic!

Children are aware of differences before they develop prejudice. For example: Your nursery-school child returns home one day with the comment "Jackie is bad. He doesn't wash." You don't know who Jackie is and question further. Your child elaborates: "He's dirty. His skin is dark all over." You, a liberal, committed to raising unbiased children, are in a state of shock. You believe that you have evidence that your own child has been exposed to racial prejudice and is on the way to becoming a bigot. You begin a lecture on equality and democracy. But is your child's comment really evidence of a developing bias? Has she told you that she considers Jackie an inferior child? Or is she merely trying to account for differences among groups, and has associated dark with dirty?

This scene is not confined to white families. Alvin Poussaint, a psychiatrist at the Harvard Medical School, presents a similar case: "... one black mother went into a tizzy because her six-year-old called his skin color 'dirty' and wanted to know why the dirt didn't wash off. This mother was thrown into a turmoil because she feared that her child was developing a 'negative identity.' She succeeded in frightening the child and increasing his tension and confusion over skin color. The child was searching for an explanation, and in his own way showing curiosity normal for a six-year-old child."

In both cases, a simple explanation is called for: that dark skin, like white skin, can be clean or dirty, that dark skin remains dark no matter how clean it is. If your child is interested, you could comment further about the similarity of skin regardless of pigment: it covers the body, can get poison ivy, can itch, bleed, needs Band-Aids, and so forth. The black parent might add, "You have a pretty brown color like Mommy and Daddy."

Black youngsters' question "Why can't I be white?" may

have a hidden agenda. It may be a question designed for a purpose, perhaps to hurt their parents in their anger over another issue, or perhaps to evoke a strong and emotional response from them. Or they might be expressing a wish to look like particular friends. Does this necessarily mean that they reject blackness? Some children may have been exposed to name calling or other forms of racial hostility, and parents should question their children about such experiences. Poussaint suggests that you not overreact, but remain supportive. Tell your children that their skin, hair, and features are attractive though different from Caucasian features. And be sure that your children are exposed to black heroes, role models, and friends.

2. Don't panic even when you hear a child's question or statement that turns out to be motivated by prejudice. Your child will not necessarily become a bigot. Early experience is important, but children are malleable, and even adults are capable of changing their attitudes.

In addition, don't feel guilty about your child's prejudicial attitudes — you may not be responsible for them. There are certainly many sources outside the home that offer negative stereotypes of different groups.

3. Take action. In other chapters we have stressed the parent's role as respondent to children's questions. With prejudice the roles might well be reversed, the parent becoming the active questioner and initiator of discussions. Don't wait until your children touch on the topic of prejudice. Prepare them by alerting them to its existence. Cast doubt on the negative stereotypes your children acquire outside of the home by asking, "What makes you say that these people are funny-looking (lazy, disgusting, stingy, inferior)?" Encourage your children to have contact with children different from themselves, such as the handicapped — easy to do now that they've come out of the closet into the classroom.

Engage your children in discussions when the topic of prejudice comes up. Wait until they're free, however, and you can command their full attention; don't do it while their favorite TV program is on. Help them become informed about particular groups. Go to the library and find books they can understand.

Special Guidelines for Questions About the Handicapped

Make clear to your child that:

1. People are the same but also different.

2. How people look or the way their disability makes them act is not the only important thing about them.

3. Each handicapped person is different from other handicapped persons.

4. There are many reasons for a handicap. Stress that a handicap is never the result of a punishment for being bad.

5. The handicapped, like the nonhandicapped, have a full range of feelings and other human characteristics.

"... I managed to see that cripples could be comely, charming, ugly, lovely, stupid, brilliant — just like all other people," wrote F. Carling, author of *And Yet We Are Human*. "And I discovered that I was able to hate or love a cripple in spite of his handicap."

Older children can understand the various causes of handicaps and how mechanical aids are used — hearing aids, wheelchairs, recordings for the blind, and so on. They can also read biographies of important handicapped people, such as Helen Keller, examine their attitudes toward others, and be aware of their own fears.

Often the subject can be dealt with incidentally and informally as questions arise. Or, if questions don't arise, you might call your children's attention to a handicapped child or adult, talk about what it must be like to sit in a wheelchair, to be blind or deaf. Help your children learn how disabled people compensate for defects in order to lead relatively normal lives.

Questions

How do you get to be blind (or deaf, or crippled)?

"Some people are born that way, others are hurt in accidents or have had an illness. They are like us in most ways, but they can't see [or hear, or move]."

If you're blind, you can't watch TV, right?

"Blind people can't watch the picture on TV but they can hear the words and the music. They read by a special touch system called Braille, in which each letter is raised from the paper. They can also write by pushing a stylus over special paper, which raises the Braille letters. There are also recordings of books for the blind, and they can learn as well as people who can see."

If you're deaf, how do you learn to speak? Do you have to go to a special school?

"Most of us learn to speak by hearing and imitating others. You are right, the deaf need special teachers to help them, but they can learn to speak, because there is nothing wrong with their voice box.

"Deaf people in the United States also have a language all their own, called American Sign Language. They learn to move their lips and at the same time move their fingers. On TV news is sometimes translated into American Sign Language. Watch it sometime."

How do you go to the bathroom if you're in a wheelchair?

"People in wheelchairs can lift themselves out, and some can stand or walk a little. There are bathrooms that have bars on the sides of the toilet, so that people can hold on to them."

What is a retard?

" 'Retarded' means learning more slowly than most children, but 'retard' has become a bad name for these children. They get angry when they're called names."

There is a kid in my class like that. The other kids call him "retard" and he gets mad and hits them. Could I become a retard?

"Most retarded children are slower to develop as babies. You're developing like most other kids and you won't become retarded."

There is this other kid who is a nut. Yesterday he went to the back of the classroom with a pair of scissors and cut a square out of his new leather jacket. What's the matter with him?

"He may be an emotionally handicapped child, who has special problems. He may be moody or have temper outbursts. Some children like that are very aggressive and get into fights all the time, and others are very quiet and don't talk to anybody. In any case, it isn't a good idea to call him a 'nut.' Whatever bothers him isn't really his fault and you'll hurt his feelings by calling him names."

Special Guidelines for Questions About the Elderly

Parents who love their own parents can easily answer questions about grandparents. Unfortunately, not all parent-grandparent, or grandchild-grandparent, relationships are trouble-free. Family discord sometimes breaks out when the child refuses to visit grandparents, or to call them on the telephone, or to be sufficiently attentive to them. You will have to answer the question "Why do I have to visit them?" — often an expression of rebellion against the parents rather than the grandparents — depending on the particular circumstances. An appeal not to hurt people's feelings frequently works, provided the child is old enough to understand reciprocity in human relationships.

Obviously, younger children need simple answers. Since

ideas involving time are complicated for them, you cannot assume that young children understand the aging process any more than they understand other processes continuing over time: education, pregnancy, justice. Actually, when they see their grandparents often, few children will ask questions about them, since they are usually accustomed to whatever the grandparents do and take them for granted. Even when elderly behavior is noted it is accepted: "My grandpa and I, we go to the movies. I watch and he snores."

The older child's questions about changes that come with age are best answered with an emphasis on the inevitability of aging for all of us. Mention that every one of us will become part of the minority of elderly people someday. Clarify that the elderly are more like other people than they are different, despite their different appearance. Encourage contact between the elderly and the young.

Many children's questions will have hidden agendas and aim at reassurance about the continued life of one or both of the grandparents, and about yours as well. (See the chapter on death.)

Questions are often about grandparents' life in "the olden days," and may be disguised curiosity about the child's mother's or father's childhood. "Grandparents know a lot of things about your parents that your parents would never tell you about" was how one eight-year-old explained the function of grandparents.

Questions

Most questions about the elderly come from older children. Try to use the same explanation but with simpler words for the younger child.

What do old people do when they don't go to work or to school?

"Some leave their jobs, retire, and do things they've always wanted to do and didn't have time for. They plant their garden, play music, spend more time with their friends or family, or start a new hobby. Some other old people feel that they have no place anywhere, that their families don't need them anymore, and they become depressed, lonely, and angry." (You might describe an actual old person the child knows, or encourage your child to talk to an old person.)

What does senile *mean? Do all old people become senile?*

"Very few become senile. But, as people get older, they become more forgetful. Some of them become confused at times, but it's usually owing to the normal slowing down that comes with age, and not because of a disease of the brain, such as senility. Forgetfulness and confusion can be due to the stresses of retirement, bereavement, loss of income and social role, or due to diseases that occur at any age but that in the elderly may cause forgetfulness and confusion.

"Poverty is a particular problem of many aged people, and it's physically harder on them than on the young (cold is less bearable, they need more conveniences, they can't walk as well, etc.). The young look toward a future in which they might be richer, but the old lack that hope."

How do you feel when you get really old, like ninety?

Help your children to be empathic. Turn the question around and ask them how they might feel if all their friends had died, if they couldn't hear or walk well, if they had to leave their home to live with somebody.

Prejudice has many causes — political, economic, psychological. A major contribution to prejudice is our fear of strangers. But we are also curious about them. Numerous research projects have shown that when children — or adults — live, work, or play together in equality, they learn how similar they really are in their personal beliefs, their likes and dislikes. They discover their common humanity. Race, religion, sex, age, physical condition, and social class then become less important than similarities in personal values in determining who their friends are.

*   *   *

We don't claim to have covered the subject of children's questions. Rather, we agree with a comment attributed to John Dewey as he ended a lecture: "I've not tried to cover the subject but rather to uncover it . . ." It would be contradictory and absurd to attempt to cover a subject that by definition must remain open and tentative.

Notes

Notes

Introduction

1. David Elkind, *Children and Adolescents: Interpretative Essays on Jean Piaget* (New York: Oxford University Press, 1970), p. 31.
2. Lewis Carroll, *Alice's Adventures in Wonderland* (New York: Grosset & Dunlap, 1946), chapter 5.
3. Nicolai Chukovsky, *From Two to Five* (Berkeley, Calif.: University of California Press, 1965), p. 30.
4. Ruth Weir, *Language in the Crib* (The Hague: Mouton and Co., 1962), p. 92.

Chapter 1

7. John Dewey, "The Germ of Intellectual Curiosity," *How We Think* (Boston: Heath, 1933).
7. Infants exploring. G. W. Greenman, "Visual Behavior of Newborn Infants"; and R. L. Fantz, "Pattern Vision in Newborn Infants"; in *The Competent Infant*, ed. L. J. Stone, J. T. Smith, and L. B. Murphy (New York: Basic Books, 1973).
8. Jean Piaget, *The Origins of Intelligence in Children* (New York: International University Press, 1956), p. 339.
8. Structure of children's questions. Philip Dale, *Language Development: Structure and Function* (New York: Holt, Rinehart and Winston, 1976).

9. Chukovsky, *From Two to Five.*
10. Dewey, *How We Think,* p. 24.
11. Jean Piaget, *The Language and Thought of the Child* (London: Routledge and Kegan Paul, 1960).
12. Sigmund Freud, *The Sexual Enlightenment of Children* (New York: Macmillan, 1963).

Chapter 2
20. Sonne Lemke, "Children's Identity Concepts" (Ph.D. dissertation, University of California, Berkeley, 1973).
21. Anne Bernstein and Philip Cowan, "Children's Concepts of How People Get Babies," *Child Development* 46 (1975), pp. 77–91.
22. Five-year-old Michelle. Ruth Formanek and Anita Gurian, *Piagetian Concepts for Clinicians* (New York: Psychotherapy Tape Club, 1977).
26. Freud, *Sexual Enlightenment.*
31. Richard Robertiello. Nancy Friday, *My Mother/My Self* (New York: Delacorte Press, 1977), p. 112.
32. Sol Gordon, *Let's Make Sex a Household Word: A Guide for Parents and Children* (New York: John Day Co., 1975).
41. Joae Graham Selzer, *When Children Ask about Sex* (Beacon Press, Boston, 1974).
47. William Block, *What Your Child Really Wants to Know about Sex and Why* (Garden City, N.Y.: Doubleday, 1970), p. 203.

Chapter 3
48. 1976 study. United States Department of Commerce, *Current Population Reports.* "Some Recent Changes in American Families," Special Studies Series P-23, No. 52 (Washington, D.C.: Bureau of the Census).
49. Judith Wallerstein and Joan Kelly, "The Effects of Parental Divorce: Experiences of the Child in Early Latency," *American Journal of Orthopsychiatry,* January 1976; "The Effects of Parental Divorce: The Adolescent Experience," in *The Child in His Family; Children at Psy-*

chiatric Risk, ed. E. J. Anthony and C. Koupernik (New York: John Wiley, 1974); "The Effects of Parental Divorce: Experience of the Preschool Child," *Journal of the American Academy of Child Psychiatry* 14 (1975), No. 4; "The Effects of Parental Divorce: Experiences of the Child in Later Latency," *American Journal of Orthopsychiatry,* April 1976.

50.   Richard Gardner, *Psychotherapy with Children of Divorce* (New York: Jason Aronson, Inc., 1976).

53.   Gilbert Kliman, *Psychological Emergencies of Childhood* (New York: Grune and Stratton, 1968), p. 98.

55.   Children's statements. D. Kavanaugh, ed., *Listen to Us: The Children's Express Report* (New York: Workman Publishing, 1978).

60.   Rita Turow, *Daddy Doesn't Live Here Anymore* (Matteson, Ill.: Great Lakes Living Press, 1977), p. 8.

74.   Louise Despert, *Children of Divorce* (New York: Doubleday, 1953), p. 117.

Chapter 4

75.   Brenda Maddox, *The Half-Parent* (New York: M. Evans, 1975), p. 16.

76.   Jessie Bernard, *Remarriage: A Study of Marriage* (New York: Russell & Russell, 1961).

76.   Children's statements. *Listen to Us,* ed. Kavanaugh.

84.   Paul Bohannon, *Divorce and After* (Englewood Cliffs, N.J.: Prentice-Hall, 1972).

87.   Norman Paget and Paul Thierry, "Adoptive Parent Education," *Children Today,* March–April 1976.

93.   Freud, *Sexual Enlightenment.*

94.   Erik H. Erikson, *Childhood and Society* (New York: Norton, 1950).

100.   Jill Robinson, *Perdido* (New York: Knopf, 1978), p. 199.

100.   Babette Dalshimer, "Adoption Runs in My Family," *Ms.,* August 1973.

100.   David Kirk, *Shared Fate* (New York: Free Press, 1964).

108.   Robinson, *Perdido,* p. 193.

109. Birth-parents' attitudes. Arthur Sorosky, Annette Baran, and Reuben Pannor, *The Adoption Triangle* (Garden City, N.Y.: Doubleday, 1978), p. 51.

110. Albert Kadushin, *Adopting Older Children* (New York: Columbia University Press, 1970).

112. Lucille Grow and Deborah Shapiro, *Black Children, White Families: A Study of Transracial Adoption* (New York: Child Welfare League of America, 1974).

115. James Comer and Alvin Poussaint, *Black Child Care* (New York: Simon and Schuster, 1975).

Chapter 6

117. Selma Fraiberg, *The Magic Years* (New York: Charles Scribner's Sons, 1959), p. 273.

118. Children identify with pets. Ruth Formanek, "When Children Ask About Death," *Elementary School Journal* 75 (1974), pp. 92–97.

119. Nursery school children's experiences with death. Kliman, *Psychological Emergencies*, p. 3.

119. Edwin Schneidman, "You and Death," *Psychology Today*, June 1971.

121. Robert Kastenbaum, "Childhood: The Kingdom Where Creatures Die," *Journal of Clinical Child Psychology* 3 (1974), pp. 11–13.

122. Liv Ullmann, *Changing* (New York, Knopf, 1977), p. 12.

125. Maria Nagy, "The Child's Theories Concerning Death," *Journal of Genetic Psychology* 73 (1948), pp. 3–27.

127. Humberto Nagera, "Children's Reactions to the Death of Important Objects: A Developmental Approach," *Psychoanalytic Study of the Child* (New York: International University Press, 1970).

129. Martha Wolfenstein, "How Is Mourning Possible?" *Psychoanalytic Study of the Child*, 1966, pp. 93–123.

129. Iona Opie and Peter Opie, *The Lore and Language of School Children* (London: Oxford University Press, 1959).

129. Len Chaloner, "How to Answer the Questions Children Ask About Death," *Parents Magazine*, November 1962.

138. Marjorie Mitchell, *The Child's Attitude Toward Death* (New York: Schocken Books, 1967), pp. 47–49.

Chapter 7

140. William Damon, *The Social World of the Child* (San Francisco: Jossey and Bass, 1977).
142. Interviews. Jean Piaget, *The Moral Judgment of the Child* (New York: Collier, 1962).
144. Steffi and Martin, in *Listen to Us*, ed. Kavanaugh.
144. E. Diener, A. L. Beaman, S. Frazer, and R. T. Kelem, "Effects of Deindividuation Variables on Stealing among Halloween Trick-or-Treaters," *Journal of Personality and Social Psychology* 33 (1976), pp. 178–83.
146. Haim G. Ginott, *Between Parent and Child* (New York: Avon Books, 1969).
148. D. W. Winnicott, *Collected Papers* (London: Tavistock Publications, 1958).
149. Piaget, *Moral Judgment*.
149. Children's statements. *Listen to Us*, ed. Kavanaugh.

Chapter 8

154. Ideas of number. Jean Piaget and Aline Szeminska, *The Child's Conception of Number* (New York: Norton, 1965).
154. Children's ideas of money. Anselm Strauss, "The Development and Transformation of Monetary Meanings in the Child," *American Journal of Sociology* 17 (1952), p. 275.
155. Interview with Tracy. Hans Furth, Mary Baur, and Janet Smith, "Children's Conception of Social Institutions: A Piagetian Framework," *Human Development* 19 (1976), pp. 351–74.
157. Scott Ward, Daniel B. Wackman, and Ellen Wartella, *How Children Learn to Buy* (Beverly Hills, Calif.: Sage Publications, 1977).
158. Helen Marshall and Lucille Magruder, "Relations between Parent Money-Education Practices and Children's Knowledge and Use of Money," *Child Development* 31 (1960), pp. 253–84.

163. Ranking occupations. Barbara Gunn, "Children's Conception of Occupational Prestige," *Personnel and Guidance Journal* 42 (1964), pp. 558–63.
167. Studs Terkel, *Hard Times: An Oral History of the Great Depression* (New York: Pantheon Books, 1970).

Chapter 9

171. George Kaluger and Clifford J. Kolson, "The Speaking Religious Vocabulary of Kindergarten Children," *Religious Education* 58 (1963), p. 387.
172. David Elkind, "The Child's Conception of His Religious Denomination: The Jewish Child," *Journal of Genetic Psychology* 99 (1961), pp. 209–25; Elkind, "The Child's Conception of His Religious Denomination: The Catholic Child," *Journal of Genetic Psychology* 101 (1962), pp. 185–93; Elkind, "The Child's Conception of His Religious Denomination: The Protestant Child," *Journal of Genetic Psychology* 103 (1963), pp. 291–304.
174. Pictures of God. E. Harms, "The Development of Religious Experience in Children," *American Journal of Sociology* 50 (1944), p. 112.
177. "Dear God," Eric Marshall, *Children's Letters to God* (New York: Simon and Schuster, 1966); E. Marshall and S. Hample, *God is a Good Friend to Have* (New York: Simon and Schuster, 1969).
181. Benjamin Spock, "What to Tell Your Child about God," *Redbook,* August 1978.
185. David Gross, *1001 Questions and Answers about Judaism* (New York: Doubleday, 1978).

Chapter 10

188. Judith Porter, *Black Child, White Child: The Development of Racial Attitudes* (Cambridge, Mass.: Harvard University Press, 1971).
189. Joyce Robertson, "A Mother's Observation on the Tonsillectomy of a 4-Year-Old Daughter," in *Physical Illness and Handicap in Childhood,* ed. Albert Solnit (New Haven: Yale University Press, 1977).

191. Confusions of time and space. Heinz Werner, *Comparative Psychology of Mental Development* (Chicago: Follet Pub. Co., 1948).

192. C. Seefeldt, R. Jantz, A. Galper, and K. Serock, "Children's Attitude toward the Elderly," *Educational Gerontology* 2 (1977), pp. 301–10.

193. Lillian Smith, quoted in Porter, *Black Child, White Child*.

194. Bill and Joan. Glenn McCracken and Charles E. Walcutt, *Basic Reading* (New York: Lippincott, 1973).

194. Phyllis Barnum, mentioned in "Grandmas are Stereotyped"; Glenda Daniel, in *Newsday*, Sept. 12, 1978.

194. Howard J. Ehrlich, *The Social Psychology of Prejudice* (New York: Wiley, 1973).

195. Barbara Williams, *Kevin's Grandma* (New York: Dutton, 1978).

195. Dolls. Miriam Formanek, "Women and Dolls" (unpublished).

196. George Orwell, "Boys' Weeklies," *Collection of Essays* (New York: Doubleday, 1954).

197. Alvan Poussaint, "Black Child," *Parents Magazine*, October 1976.

199. F. Carling, *And Yet We Are Human* (London: Chatto and Windus, 1962).

203. M. Brewster Smith, "The Schools and Prejudice," *Social Psychology and Human Values: Selected Essays by M. Brewster Smith* (Chicago: Aldine, 1969).